Addressing the Bard

stroan

thrawed and tholed

birl

thrawn

Matthew Fitt • Seamus Heaney • W.N. Herbert
Carol Ann Duffy • James Robertson • Tim Turnbull • Rab Wilson
Meg Bateman • Robert Crawford • Liz Lochhead • Janet Paisley
Jackie Kay

Addressing the Bard:

twelve contemporary poets respond to Robert Burns

edited by Douglas Gifford

First published in 2009 by
Scottish Poetry Library
5 Crichton's Close
Edinburgh
EH8 8DT
www.spl.org.uk

ISBN 978-0-9532235-9-6
Introduction and editorial matter
copyright © Scottish Poetry
Library 2009
Individual poems copyright ©
the authors 2009

Seamus Heaney, 'A Birl for
Burns', reprinted from *A Night
Out with Robert Burns*, edited by
Andrew O'Hagan (Canongate,
2008) by kind permission of the
publishers.

Design and illustrations
copyright © Iain McIntosh 2009

Printed and bound in West
Yorkshire, England by
The Charlesworth Group

The Scottish Poetry Library
acknowledges the support of
Learning and Teaching Scotland,
Scottish Qualifications Authority
and the Scottish Arts Council in
the publication of this book.

*The Scottish Poetry Library
is particularly grateful to the
Andrew Dickson Memorial
Fund for its generous support
for the publication of this
book. For Andrew, poetry was
a part of daily life and he
would have applauded this
book's attempt to make it just
that for a wider audience.*

Contents

Burns in a New Millennium

The 250th anniversary of the birth of Robert Burns is a year of celebration of the poet's life and work. But this Year of Homecoming also presents challenges, particularly for younger readers, most of whom are very distant in experience and imagination – and language – from the eighteenth-century world of rural Ayrshire. What has a young farmer, haunted by poverty, anger at the world's injustice, in love with the natural world and the beauty of women, and caught up in the complex and ferocious religious divisions of his time, to offer to teenagers at home with city life and the rich diversities of popular music, television and multi-media?

This collection of poems by Burns and some of our best modern poets is part of that celebration. A short book like this cannot hope to represent the range of his work: its aims are to let modern poets show how Burns still inspires, and how his ideas and example are still vividly alive. As the poets write about their chosen Burns poems, and how they engaged with them, it soon becomes clear, however, that their contributions – while warmly appreciative of Burns – are often unexpected and surprising, with frequent questioning of the poet, his attitudes and values. What emerges, as well as an understanding of Burns in all his moods, is a contemporary debate as to what Burns means to us now – and it is a debate which we invite you, the new readers of Burns in a new millennium, to join. Too often, perhaps, Burns is handed down to us as a Scottish stereotype: the Heaven-taught ploughman, poor, noble yet flawed, victim of his own excesses, yet speaking to Everyman (and Woman?) the world over. We can forget his father

Introduction

was something of a philosopher, he and his brother had a private tutor who went on to teach at Scotland's oldest school (still very much alive as Ayr Academy), he had almost to unlearn his polite Anglicised education from John Murdoch to discover older, indigenous Scottish writing and poetry, and that he could – in matters of religion – be very much *not* of the people as he argued against the passionately held right of ordinary Scottish people to choose their own ministers which he likened to giving cattle the right to choose their herds. He could swither between supporting French revolution and condemning it; he died of rheumatic heart disease, not drink. How dangerously mythology distorts the picture of an extremely complex and all too human genius!

So – explore these addresses to our Bard; but argue about the poems, by Burns and the moderns. Try to read his poems fresh, before reading what other poets say about them, and see if you agree. Speak them – so that the wonderful and natural speaking voice of Burns comes alive, and so that his old and expressive Scots words come alive, too. Talk about your favourites in class – and maybe, as Matthew Fitt suggests, try writing some of your own – and don't just use your usual standard English, but try using the kind of Scots you still speak, or find out words used by friends and relatives from Aberdeen to Galashiels, Glasgow to Dundee. Don't forget that when he wanted different effects, Burns could write in beautiful standard English too – try and find some of these passages in the poems here (hint: the middle of 'Tam o' Shanter').

There is a pattern to this book

(although you may well wish to create your own). When we knew what poems our modern poets had chosen, we decided to begin with Burns at home in his immediate world, a world not just of farming and natural beauty, but of the mouse, the louse and his favourite sheep, Mailie; to move on to his letter-poems ('Epistles') – the first to a brother poet, Davie, the second, advice to the young son of a friend; then, to the poet in and on love in 'Mary Morison', 'A red red Rose', and 'John Anderson my Jo'. But Burns was more than one of the world's great love poets and song-writers; his acute intelligence focused on the larger history of Scotland, and its religious and political follies and cruelties. So we have that great exhortation of Bruce to his troops on his march to Bannockburn in 1314, 'Scots, wha hae wi' Wallace bled'; we have what is possibly the world's finest exposure of a pompous and selfish hypocrite, whose nickname has become legendary, in 'Holy Willie's Prayer', where Burns so marvellously adopts the voice of all that he despises and hates in religious bigotry. We have another satire, this time on cruel aristocracy and the way it all too often regarded its tenants as cattle, in the 'Address of Beelzebub' – again, Burns puts on a voice as far from his own as could be imagined, that of the Prince of Darkness, Satan's right-hand man, as he encourages Scottish aristocrats to even greater cruelty.

As we follow Burns from Ayr to the wider worlds of religion and politics, our modern poets follow, each writing a response-poem to their choice of Burns, and telling us what they find to inspire them. They can speak for themselves – it is enough for me to repeat here that they constantly surprise, seeing Burns anew, just as we hope that you will find your own Burns fresh, and constantly connecting with our modern world. See how Liz Lochhead questions whether Burns is really writing about the

mouse, or rather drawing attention to himself and his sensitivity. Do you agree, or are there other ways to read the poem, for example seeing the mouse as representing all homeless, poor creatures, animal and human? When Burns attacks the louse which climbs in the would-be fashionable Jenny's hair, is it the louse he is mocking, or something and someone else? Tim Turnbull's version of 'To a Louse' neatly turns the tables on Burns by suggesting that Burns's famous phrase 'to see ourselves as other see us', if applied to himself might give him at the least a violent headache! And at the heart of his comment lies the million-dollar question – *But who is he?* – which scholars and readers have endlessly debated.

The modern poets' questioning continues, as Bill Herbert's commentary celebrates Burns's language, and his controlled spontaneity – but has his own 'Epistle' send up in glorious surrealism the Burns cult, with Haggismen and 'waant tae be' Robins, would-be poets following Burns, coming alive once a year at the dead of winter – while for the rest of the year the Scots language is ignored. Robert Crawford cuts closer to Burns himself in commenting on the 'Epistle to a Young Friend'; can you find what he finds in the poem, where Burns's life seems to contradict his advice? Does this lessen the poem's value?

At the centre of our selection lie three wonderful poems of love – and not just romantic love. Indeed, hasn't love of various kinds been a theme of all the poems by Burns *and* the modern poets so far, in the sense that care and affection for humanity and animals shine through all? With Carol Ann Duffy, Matthew Fitt and Jackie Kay responding to 'Mary Morison', 'A red red Rose', and 'John Anderson' we are at the heart of Burns and some of the world's simplest and greatest love poetry – yet even here our modern poets shed new light. Why do you think Duffy calls her ghostly poem 'Sung'? Is her message simply that all love dies? Is Matthew Fitt's caustic city exchange between youngsters mocking Burns's feelings as irrelevant to the modern urban world – or is something else going on? (Watch for that surprise last line...) And, responding to Burns and 'John Anderson', notice how Jackie Kay tells us that she leaves out the name of her friend in 'Fiere',

her evocation of a life's friendship, so that every reader can join in such a celebration.

Then come three poets who project Burns and his universal themes on to world issues today. Janet Paisley uses Burns's ideas of courage against tyranny in the time of Bruce to relate to her own personal confrontations in 'Aw Jock Tamson's', and then argues that we must all recover courage and integrity in the financial and moral crises of today. (Her title draws on the Scots proverb that says that we're all Jock Tamson's bairns – that is, we all come from an ancient single father, and that we thus belong to common humanity. Why does she leave out 'bairns' from her title?)

Even fiercer in their attack on the way the modern world is going are Rab Wilson's 'Holy Gordon's Prayer' and James Robertson's 'Beelzebub Resurfaces'; the first controversially remaking the eighteenth-century bigot into a Scottish Prime Minister, and attacking his political colleagues and by implication, the corruption Wilson sees (like Paisley) at the heart of our society; and the second rediscovering, as Burns did, the devil from Hell finding himself once again delighted by man's inhumanity to man – and, for Robertson, to the planet.

Also at the heart of our poets' responses to Burns is the issue of language. We have English, Gaelic and Scots – but implied throughout is an emphasis on freedom of language, so that Scots can move into English and back, just as it does in many of the Burns poems here. You will find if you read the poems out loud that your tone, accent and language will frequently change, in tune with the effects the poets want – of love, pretension and snobbery, bigotry, mockery, and reflection, thoughtful or sad. And there is no single standard of Scots in the modern poems; rather it is by turns traditional, urban and still evolving (in words like 'scoobie' and 'barrie' and 'retro-wedgie'), changing according to whether it's

Glasgow or Dundee Scots. Poets make their own language, and refuse to be told what language to use!

This little anthology is the tip of an iceberg. You could follow up from here by reading wonderful Burns poems such as 'The Jolly Beggars', 'The Holy Fair', 'Hallowe'en', and matchless songs such as 'Ae Fond Kiss' and 'The Banks and Braes o' Doon'. You could also follow up the work of the modern poets you particularly enjoyed here. And while the collection's aim is to encourage younger secondary school students to discover Burns and some contemporary poets, we hope that senior pupils, their teachers and a wider audience can enjoy these poems too. Finally, it is worth noting that a selection of Burns poems is now prescribed for Advanced Higher, so this volume may help in leading students towards further study.

What emerges from all these poems is that Burns still speaks directly to the present, and that while names, places and issues may change, the underlying corruptions and outrages of the world continue to demand anger and satire on behalf of ordinary humanity. You will find further commentary in the Notes at the end together with a glossary for the modern poets' Scots. But first, enjoy the variety, skill and passion of Burns and our modern poets' responses.

DOUGLAS GIFFORD
University of Glasgow 2009

To a Mouse, On turning her up in her Nest, with the Plough, November, 1785

WEE, sleeket, cowran, tim'rous *beastie*,   sleek, cowering
O, what a panic's in thy breastie!
Thou need na start awa sae hasty,
        Wi' bickering brattle!   scurrying rush
I wad be laith to rin an' chase thee,   loath
        Wi' murd'ring *pattle*!   small spade to clean the plough

I'm truly sorry Man's dominion
Has broken Nature's social union,
An' justifies that ill opinion,
        Which makes thee startle,
At me, thy poor, earth-born companion,
        An' *fellow-mortal*!

I doubt na, whyles, but thou may *thieve*;   sometimes
What then? poor beastie, thou maun live!
A *daimen-icker* in a *thrave*   occasional ear of corn among two stooks
        'S a sma' request:
I'll get a blessin wi' the lave,   rest, what's left
        An' never miss 't!

Thy wee-bit *housie*, too, in ruin!
It's silly wa's the win's are strewin!
An' naething, now, to big a new ane,   build
        O' foggage green!   rough green grass
An' bleak *December's winds* ensuin,
        Baith snell an' keen!   both sharp and keen

Thou saw the fields laid bare an' wast,
An' weary *Winter* comin fast,
An' cozie here, beneath the blast,   cosy
        Thou thought to dwell,
Till crash! the cruel *coulter* past   blade on the plough
        Out thro' thy cell.

That wee-bit heap o' leaves an' stibble,   stubble
Has cost thee monie a weary nibble!
Now thou's turn'd out, for a' thy trouble,
                But house or hald,   without house or smallholding
To thole the Winter's *sleety dribble*,
                An' *cranreuch* cauld!   frosty

But Mousie, thou art no thy-lane,   alone
In proving *foresight* may be vain:
The best laid schemes o' *Mice* an' *Men*,
                Gang aft agley,   go often askew, adrift
An' lea'e us nought but grief an' pain,   leave
                For promis'd joy!

Still, thou art blest, compar'd wi' *me*!
The *present* only toucheth thee:
But Och! I *backward* cast my e'e,
                On prospects drear!
An' *forward*, tho' I canna *see*,
                I *guess* an' *fear*!

Liz Lochhead

From a Mouse

*The present author being, from her mother's milk, a lover of the
poetic effusions of Mr Robert Burns and all creatures therein
(whether mouse, louse, yowe, dug or grey mare Meg) was
nonetheless appalled to find, in her slattern's kitchen, sitting up
washing its face in her wok, the following phenomenon:*

It's me. The eponymous *the moose*
The *To a Mouse* that – were I in your hoose,
A bit o dust ablow the bed, thon dodd o' oose
That, quick, turns tail,
Is – eek! – a *livin creature* on the loose,
Wad gar you wail.

Aye, I've heard you fairly scraich, you seem
Gey phobic 'boot Mice in Real Life yet dream
Aboot Man-Mouse Amity? Ye'll rhyme a ream!
Yet, wi skirt wrapt roon,
I've seen ye staun up oan a chair an scream
Like Daphne Broon.

But I'm *adored* – on paper! – ever since
First ye got me at the schule, at yince
Enchantit – wha'd aye thocht poetry was *mince*
Till ye met Rabbie,
My poor, earth-born companion, an the prince
O *Standard Habbie*.

For yon is what they cry the form *he* wrote in
An' *you* recite. Gey easy, as you ken, to quote in
Because it *sticks*. I will allow it's *stoatin*,
This nifty stanza
He could go to sicc lengths wi, say sicc a lot in –
Largs to Lochranza,

Plockton to Peebles, Dumfries to Dundee,
If a wean kens ony poem aff by hert, it's *Me!*
Will greet ower ma plough-torn nest, no see
The bit o' a gap
Atween the fause Warld o' Poetry
An baited trap.

Get Rentokil! Get real! Wha you love
'S the *ploughman* in the poem, keen to prove
– Saut tears, sigh, sympathy – he's *sensitive*.
Wee sermon:
Mice, men, schemes agley, Himsel' above
Cryin me *Vermin*.

Ploughman? That will be right! *Heaven-taught?*
He drank deep o The Bard, and Gray, and Pope – the lot.
I, faur frae the spontaneous outburst you thought,
Am an *artifact*.
For Man's Dominion he was truly sorry? Not!
'T was all an act.

Burns, baith man and poet, liked to dominate.
His reputation wi the lassies wasna great.
They *still* dinna ken whether they love to hate,
Or hate to love.
He was *'an awfy man!'* He left them tae their fate,
Push came to shove.

Couldnae keep it in his breeks? Hell's bells, damnation,
I wad be the vera last to gie a peroration
On the daft obsession o this prurient Nation,
His amatory antics.
He was – beating them tae it by a generation –
First o th' Romantics.

Arguably I am a poem wha, prescient, did presage
Your Twentyfirst Century Global Distress Age.
I'm a female *mouse* though, he didna give a sausage
For ma sparklin een!
As for Mother Nature? Whether yez get the message
Remains to be seen.

This is just a wee parody written out of my
enduring love for the original. The first Burns poem which, fifty
years ago, when I was ten, I learned off by heart to recite it at the
200th Anniversary Burns Competition in the Miners' Welfare Hall.
(See, I wasn't a good enough singer to be allowed to do 'Ye Banks and
Braes' or 'Ca the Yowes' or 'Flow Gently Sweet Afton'...) Our village
– an old mining village turned into a scheme, post-war housing for the
nearby industrial town of Motherwell in Lanarkshire – had lots of what
they always called 'Burns Afficionados' among the working men, the
steelmen and the miners and the joiners and the shopkeepers; great
enthusiasts for 'our national bard' among our teachers and our parents.
    A parody, the sincerest form of flattery, a wee bit of fun. But I
was trying to laugh at myself and my own hypocrisy at loving the mouse
in the poem and being so afraid of the wee creatures in real life – I do
stand on chairs and scream like a woman in a comic! And I wanted to
do this in a very imperfect version of 'Burns Stanza' – or 'Standard
Habbie' as it's known. My lines (I tell myself it's for comic effect) tend

to be two syllables, or an extra stress, too long – and you're really not supposed to run a sentence on into the next stanza, as I do between four and five. The form properly demands to be 'end-stopped' and for the sense units and the verses to go hand in hand.

I wanted this mouse to see through human beings and, in its own voice, talk back, take the mickey (aargh, no pun intended) out of Scotsmen – and Scotswomen – who sentimentalise Burns as a simple 'heaven-taught ploughman'. Whereas, although he was always poor and did work long and hard and unsuccessfully at farming, still he was very thoroughly, if largely *self*-educated, incredibly widely read. And I especially wanted to satirise our partial and prurient interest in his life and loves and personality rather than concentrating on the *words he wrote*. Which are the whole point. So varied in tone and register, they go brilliantly swooping, sometimes within the one poem, from high to low, from posh English to intimate Ayrshire dialect with such sophistication, confidence, brio, tenderness, intimacy, humour – and, whiles, frankly relished coorseness.

'To a Mouse' – though it's about a dozen or twenty years before its time – could, arguably, be the first poem of the Romantic era. It's easy to see why Wordsworth and Keats – and Byron – admired Burns so much. It's also a very 'green' poem, for our time.

I enjoyed the list of animals, the mixture of English and Scots, in the imitation eighteenth-century prose prologue from 'the author of this poem' – who is not me, though I do, I'm afraid, have a slattern's kitchen. And a wok... No mice, though. Stay away!

LIZ LOCHHEAD

To a Louse, On Seeing one on a Lady's Bonnet at Church

Ha! whare ye gaun, ye crowlan ferlie!   *crawling wonder*
Your impudence protects you sairly:
I canna say but ye strunt rarely,   *swagger, strut*
         Owre *gawze* and *lace*;   *over*
Tho' faith, I fear ye dine but sparely,
         On sic a place.

Ye ugly, creepan, blastet wonner,   *accursed, blasted; wonder*
Detested, shunn'd, by saunt an' sinner,   *saint*
How daur ye set your fit upon her,   *foot*
         Sae fine a *Lady*!
Gae somewhere else and seek your dinner,
         On some poor body.

Swith, in some beggar's haffet squattle;   *away!; squat in some beggar's sidelocks*
There ye may creep, and sprawl, and sprattle,   *scramble*
Wi' ither kindred, jumping cattle,   *lice, animals in general*
         In shoals and nations;
Whare *horn* nor *bane* ne'er daur unsettle,   *horn or bone comb; never dare disturb*
         Your thick plantations.

Now haud you there, ye're out o' sight,   *stay there*
Below the fatt'rels, snug and tight,   *ribbon ends*
Na faith ye yet! ye'll no be right,   *No, confound you*
         Till ye've got on it,
The vera tapmost, towrin height
         O' *Miss's bonnet*.

My sooth! right bauld ye set your nose out,   *really!*
As plump an' gray as onie grozet: *any gooseberry*
O for some rank, mercurial rozet,   *resin or drug containing mercury*

      Or fell, red smeddum,   *strong red powder (medicinal)*
I'd gie you sic a hearty dose o't,
        Wad dress your droddum!   *thrash your backside!*

I wad na been surpriz'd to spy
You on an auld wife's *flainen toy*;   *flannel cap*
Or aiblins some bit duddie boy,   *perhaps; small ragged*
        On 's *wylecoat*;   *flannel vest*
But Miss's fine *Lunardi*, fye!   *bonnet (named after the*
        How daur ye do 't?   *famous Italian balloonist)*

O *Jenny* dinna toss your head,
An' set your beauties a' abroad!   *all abroad*
Ye little ken what cursed speed
        The blastie's makin!   *nasty beast*
Thae *winks* and *finger-ends*, I dread,   *gesticulations*
        Are notice takin!   *causing notice!*

O wad some Pow'r the giftie gie us
To see oursels as others see us!
It wad frae monie a blunder free us
        An' foolish notion:
What airs in dress an' gait wad lea'e us,   *fashion*
        And ev'n Devotion!   *even false piety*

Tim Turnbull

To a Louse

Ahoy there, prince of parasites!
At risk of giving you a fright,
you have been, estimable mite,
   immortalised,
and scaled to literary heights.
   Are you surprised?

Your own bloodthirsty tribe, I know's
turned up *en masse* in verse and prose
by the likes of Rosenberg, Rimbaud,
   and George Orwell.
Not one's so celebrated, though,
   as your guid sel.

Yer lad's there in the pew behind
with farmer's boots and hands. You'll find,
(the plough-boy thing's a pose), his mind
   is like a whip –
swift, sharp and ready with a rhyme,
   or cutting quip:

songs to scourge the landlord classes,
to make you weep or charge your glasses,
hymn Nature or exalt the masses
          in plaint or racket,
or warm his way into some lass's
          starchy placket

(this last we know with some success
as parish registers attest),
and in his hands, dear household pest,
          you become huge:
a stand-in for the dispossessed
          and comic's stooge.

But who is he? I hear you ask.
To find out that's a fulltime task
so varied were his moods and masks,
          so broad his muse,
you'd have to get yourself a desk
          at St Andrew's –

a Socialist *avant la lettre*,
a folk revivalist and setter,
a proto-Thatcherite go-getter,
          sell-out Blackguard,
British Romantic (only better),
          SCOTIA's BARD:

to see himself as others see him,
would frankly, Lousy, likely gie him
schizophrenia or at least, a megrim,
          which begs the thought,
You wouldn't really want to be him.
          Well, maybe not.

Robert Burns is one of those writers whose ubiquity (even in England) can lead you to think that you know them and their work better than you actually do. I remember Burns songs being played on the radio and the poems cropping up at school, college and on television.

He's also eminently quotable, so he crops up out of context all over the place. I had a sketchy idea about his life (farmer, rake, excise man, died young) but not the full picture. When I was asked to write this poem I thought I'd better remedy that.

The first thing you notice is that there isn't a definitive Burns – or at least, different ages tend to reinvent him in their own image. So he becomes at various times a poet of sentiment, love, nationalism (Scottish or British) or radicalism. I suppose that's true of most writers but given the extent of his popularity it seems more extreme in Burns. From his letters and contemporary accounts it's also clear that Burns himself was pretty changeable, presenting in different ways to different people, so I decided that this had to be a part of the poem.

I chose 'To a Louse' primarily because it makes me laugh. I love the idea of the lice as cattle roaming plantations of hair. The image has a cartoonish quality and the language is cacophonous – squattle, sprattle, grozet, droddum – which gives great energy to the piece. During the composition of my poem I found myself envying the richness of Burns's Scots vernacular.

There is also a sense in the original that it was written for performance. At the time of writing Burns had a ready audience of like-minded young bucks and I tried to imagine how it would be delivered and received. I found myself wondering just how sympathetic Burns really was to poor Jenny, as some commentators suggest, or if his mock-sermonizing the final stanza might be even less sincere than it appears.

I imagine if read in the kirkyard or a clubbable gathering above a pub it could sound a little like someone farting and then theatrically blaming the dog. Perhaps poor Jenny's crime is not in setting herself above the dispossessed, or of religious hypocrisy, but in making herself unavailable to Burns and his mates. That's the poem's virtue, though. It is not merely that it has layers of meaning that can be unpeeled like an onion, but that it looks slightly different depending on what angle you approach it from.

TIM TURNBULL

Poor Mailie's Elegy

LAMENT in rhyme, lament in prose,
Wi' saut tears trickling down your nose;   salt
Our *Bardie*'s fate is at a close,
      Past a' remead!   past all remedy
The last, sad cape-stane of his woes;   copestone
      Poor Mailie's dead!

It 's no the loss o' warl's gear,   wordly wealth and property
That could sae bitter draw the tear,
Or make our *Bardie*, dowie, wear   dismal
      The mourning weed:
He 's lost a friend and neebor dear,   neighbour
      In *Mailie* dead.

Thro' a' the town she trotted by him;
A lang half-mile she could descry him;
Wi' kindly bleat, when she did spy him,
      She ran wi' speed:
A friend mair faithfu' ne'er came nigh him,   near him
      Than *Mailie* dead.

I wat she was a *sheep* o' sense,   know
An' could behave hersel wi' mense: sense
I'll say 't, she never brak a fence,   broke
      Thro' thievish greed.
Our *Bardie*, lanely, keeps the spence   lonely; keeps the parlour, keeps indoors
      Sin' *Mailie*'s dead.

Or, if he wanders up the howe,   glen
Her living image in *her yowe*,   ewe
Comes bleating to him, owre the knowe,   hillock
      For bits o' bread;
An' down the briny pearls rowe   tears roll down
      For *Mailie* dead.

She was nae get o' moorlan tips,   no child of a moorland ram
Wi' tauted ket, an' hairy hips;   matted fleece
For her forbears were brought in ships,   ancestors
      Frae 'yont the TWEED:

A bonier *fleesh* ne'er cross'd the clips — fleece; shears
      Than *Mailie*'s dead.

Wae worth that man wha first did shape, — woe befall
That vile, waunchancie thing—*a raep*! — unlucky; rope
It maks guid fellows girn an' gape, — snarl and stare
      Wi' chokin dread;
An' *Robin*'s bonnet wave wi' crape — wear a mourning band (crepe)
      For *Mailie* dead.

O, a' ye *Bards* on bonie DOON!
An' wha on Aire your chanters tune! — who tune your (bag)pipes in Ayr
Come, join the malancholious croon — melancholy lament
      O' *Robin*'s reed! — pipe
His heart will never get aboon! — rejoice, revive
      His *Mailie*'s dead!

Meg Bateman

Dòbhran Marbh

Tha a' chlosach air ragachadh
mar gun robh e a' snàmh,
spliadh is ceann air an togail,
sùil is bian
a' deàrrsadh mar umha.

Tionndaidhidh mi air falbh,
air mo nàrachadh ro mheatair de
dhòbhran fom sgrùdadh,
is am bàs air biast cho falbhach
a ghlacadh.

Air ulbhaig, làrach fhuilteach
a chuinnlean; os a cionn,
sgeilp a' stobadh a-mach

de riasg 's de fhraoch
far an do thuit e

An comhair a chinn dha na creagan foidhe,
far an laigh e san dubhar mar chloich eile,
a shròn air a pronnadh, gaoisid na fhiaclan,
air a chùlaibh, a shaobhaidh, ùrail, gorm,
mun cuairt air sa bhruach, dàil-chuach is seòbhrach.

Sìnidh mo làmh gu grad thuige
's mi a' tuigsinn gun deach a nàdar
ceàrr air an drip an earraich,
gun rachadh an dòbhran mòrail
cuideachd air iomrall.

Dead Otter

Rigor-mortis curves the beast
as if in water,
flat head and webbed foot
raised, eyes gleaming,
pelt of bronze.

I turn away, embarrassed
by a metre of otter
laid out for my scrutiny,
by death's exposure
of so fleet a creature.

On a boulder, the bloody
stamp of its nostrils;
above, a jutting ledge

of tangled fibrous root
where it must have fallen

Headlong to the rocks where it lies in shade
with staved in snout and stillness of stone,
white fur gripped between its teeth,
its lair behind, lush with liverwort,
a flicker of violets and primrose in the bank.

I reach out to it, shocked,
that in the bustle of spring,
instinct could fail it,
shocked that it too
could lose its footing.

I chose to respond to 'Poor Mailie's Elegy' with my poem 'Dòbhran Marbh' (Dead Otter). Burns's poem is about the death of a sheep with which he had a special bond. She would run to him from half a mile away and accompany him all round the town. There is something of the mock elegy about this poem, with Burns exaggerating his sadness:

> Our *Bardie*'s fate is at a close,
>   Past a' remead...

and urging other poets to 'join the melancholious croon', but even so we sense how much he misses his 'friend and neebor dear'. Anyone who has lost an animal, having grown used to its faithfulness, will understand why Burns wanted to commemorate her.

My poem 'Dead Otter' also expresses regret at the accidental death of an animal, but unlike Mailie, the otter is wild. Mailie has been strangled by a rope; my otter has fallen off a cliff. While Burns laments a loss of companionship, I lament a loss of life force; his poem is an elegy, mine, more of a word-picture. In both cases, there is a sense of kinship with the animal, a recognition that humans and animals are not so very different. 'Dead Otter' moves from my embarrassment at having the opportunity to examine a very shy

animal at length to a sense of identification with the
animal, as I realise that despite their instincts, animals,
like myself, can make mistakes. To err is human, it
is said, but here I discover that it is also animal.

Burns often expresses his compassion for
animals, and it lets him recognise the animal in people,
even among the most lofty of ladies. In his time, the
church taught that man had been created separately
from animals, which were created for our use. The sort
of commonality Burns felt intuitively between all forms
of life, between mice, sheep, trees, daisies, beggars and
dukes, is increasingly borne out by modern science,
which shows we are more, not less, like other forms
of life. For example, speech used to be considered a
uniquely human attribute, but now the gene responsible
for speech has also been found, with small differences, in
dolphins, whales, bats, mice and of course birds. We read
how much genetic material we share with chimpanzees
(98 per cent), fruit-flies (60 per cent), even bananas
(50 per cent). In short, we know that all forms of life are
interrelated. The shared genome of life is vastly poetic!

I have followed Burns in trying to express
something of our affinity with animals. He does it in the
infectiously cheerful Standard Habbie stanza form, which
no doubt would have carried his friends gleefully through
his recitation of the poem's eight verses, with a mixture
of regret for Mailie's endearing ways, enjoyment of the
rhythm and rhyme, and amusement at the most meek of
animals getting such a heroic send-off. But I didn't want
to risk parodying Burns by mimicking his metre or wit. I
needed a much quieter place to observe the dead otter
and to understand my sudden rush of feeling for it.

MEG BATEMAN

Epistle to Davie, a Brother Poet

WHILE winds frae off BEN-LOMOND blaw,
And bar the doors wi' driving snaw,
   And hing us owre the ingle,   *make us hang over the fireplace, fireside*
I set me down, to pass the time,
And spin a verse or twa o' rhyme,
   In hamely, *westlin* jingle.   *homely west country rhyme*
While frosty winds blaw in the drift,
   Ben to the chimla lug,   *up to the chimney corner*
I grudge a wee the *Great-folk*'s gift,   *I resent a bit*
   That live sae bien an' snug: *prosperous and comfortable*
    I tent less, and want less   *I value less*
     Their roomy fire-side;
    But hanker and canker,   *resent and grumble*
     To see their cursed pride.

It's hardly in a body's pow'r,
To keep, at times, frae being sour,
   To see how things are shar'd;
How *best o' chiels* are whyles in want,   *best of fellows are sometimes poor*
While *Coofs* on countless thousands rant,   *fools revel in wealth*
   And ken na how to wair 't: *and don't know how to spend it*
But Davie lad, ne'er fash your head,   *trouble yourself*
   Tho' we hae little gear,   *wealth*
We're fit to win our daily bread,
   As lang 's we're hale and fier: *whole and healthy*
    'Mair spier na, nor fear na,'   *don't ask or hear any more*
     Auld age ne'er mind a feg;   *a fig, a bit*
    The last o't, the warst o't,
     Is only but to beg.

To lye in kilns and barns at e'en,   *evening*
When banes are craz'd, and bluid is thin,   *bones are cracked, stiff*
   Is, doubtless, great distress!
Yet then *content* could make us blest;
Ev'n then, sometimes we'd snatch a taste

Of truest happiness.
The honest heart that's free frae a'
    Intended fraud or guile,
However Fortune kick the ba',
    Has ay some cause to smile:
        And mind still, you'll find still,
        A comfort this nae sma';   no small comfort
        Nae mair then, we'll care then,
        Nae *farther* we can *fa'*.

What tho', like Commoners of air,
We wander out, we know not where,
    But either house or hal'?   without
Yet *Nature*'s charms, the hills and woods,
The sweeping vales, and foaming floods,
    Are free alike to all.
In days when Daisies deck the ground,
    And Blackbirds whistle clear,
With honest joy, our hearts will bound,
    To see the *coming* year:
        On braes when we please then,   hillsides
        We'll sit and *sowth* a tune;   hum
        Syne *rhyme* till 't, we'll time till 't,   then
        And sing 't when we hae done.

It 's no in titles nor in rank;
It 's no in wealth like *Lon'on Bank*,
    To purchase peace and rest;
It 's no in makin muckle, *mair*:   making a lot, more
It 's no in books; it's no in Lear,   learning
    To make us truly blest:
If Happiness hae not her seat
    And center in the breast,
We may be *wise*, or *rich*, or *great*,
    But never can be *blest*:
        Nae treasures, nor pleasures
        Could make us happy lang;
        The *heart* ay 's the part ay,
        That makes us right or wrang.

Think ye, that sic as *you* and *I*,
Wha drudge and drive thro' wet and dry,
    Wi' never-ceasing toil;
Think ye, are we less blest than they,
Wha scarcely tent us in their way,   heed
    As hardly worth their while?
Alas! how aft, in haughty mood,
    GOD's creatures they oppress!
Or else, neglecting a' that's guid,
    They riot in excess!
        Baith careless, and fearless,
          Of either Heaven or Hell;
        Esteeming, and deeming,
          It a' an idle tale!

Then lest us chearfu' acquiesce;   cheerfully agree
Nor make our scanty Pleasures less,
    By pining at our state:
And, ev'n should Misfortunes come,
I, here wha sit, hae met wi' some,   I who sit here
    An's thankfu' for them yet.   and am thankful
They gie the wit of *Age to Youth*;
    They let us ken oursel;   understand ourselves
They make us see the naked truth,
    The *real* guid and ill.
        Tho' losses, and crosses,
          Be lessons right severe,
        There's *wit* there, ye'll get there,
          Ye'll find nae other where.

But tent me, DAVIE, *Ace o' Hearts*!   heed
(To say aught less wad wrang the *cartes*,   to say anything less would
    And flatt'ry I detest)
This life has joys for you and I;
And joys that riches ne'er could buy;
    And joys the very best.
There 's a' the *Pleasures o' the Heart*,
    The *Lover* and the *Frien'*;
Ye hae your MEG, your dearest part,
    And I my darling JEAN!

It warms me, it charms me,
　　To mention but her *name*:
It heats me, it beets me,　　　　　　kindles
　　And sets me a' on flame!

O, all ye *Pow'rs* who rule above!
O THOU, whose very self art *love*!
　　　THOU know'st my words sincere!
The *life blood* streaming thro' my heart,
Or my more dear *Immortal part*,　　　i.e. his soul
　　Is not more fondly dear!
When heart-corroding care and grief
　　Deprive my soul of rest,
Her dear idea brings relief,
　　And solace to my breast.
　　　Thou BEING, Allseeing,
　　　　O hear my fervent pray'r!
　　Still take her, and make her,
　　　Thy most peculiar care!　　　particular, especial

All hail! ye tender feelings dear!
The smile of love, the friendly tear,
　　The sympathetic glow!
Long since, this world's thorny ways
Had number'd out my weary days,
　　Had it not been for you!
Fate still has blest me with a friend,
　　In ev'ry care and ill;
And oft a more *endearing* band,
　　A *tye* more tender still.
　　　It lightens, it brightens,
　　　　The tenebrific scene,　　　dark and gloomy
　　To meet with, and greet with.
　　　My DAVIE or my JEAN!

O, how that *name* inspires my style!
The words come skelpan, rank and file,　　rushing
　　Amaist before I ken!　　　almost before I know it
The ready measure rins as fine,
As *Phoebus* and the famous *Nine*

Were glowran owre my pen.
My spavet *Pegasus* will limp,   lame
     Till ance he 's fairly het;   till he's fairly heated
And then he'll hilch, and stilt, and jimp,   hobble, and prance, and jump
     And rin an unco fit: run at unusual speed
       But least then, the beast then,
         Should rue this hasty ride,
     I'll light now, and dight now,   wipe
       His sweaty, wizen'd hide.

W.N. Herbert

Epistle

Leeze me on rhyme! It's aye a treasure,
My chief, amaist my only pleasure...
from 'Second Epistle to Davie'

While London's steekit beh thi snaw
and ilka sleekit chitterin jaw
    is ettlin tae describe
hoo drifts ur white, and ice is cauld,
and feel thi lave maun be enthralled –
    Eh've Bowmore tae imbibe.
And as the nicht – mair dreh nor me –
    draas in, Eh think Eh'll scrieve
a wee epistle tae, let's see,
    thi deid and Doctor Grieve –
    auld hermits, wee MacDiarmids,
      thi ghaist o guid Lapraik:
    here's a ravie fur young Davie,
      an a rant fur Rabbie's sake.

Fur the tartan telephone is playin
'For Auld Lang Syne'; some cloud's displayin –
well, it's no quite the Batsign – weans
    wull hae nae clue,
but aa thir dominies are prayin
    tae Burns's Ploo.

Some anniversary or ither
huz gote thi lot tae plot thigither
and ask frae whaur – Stranraer? – or whither
    remeid sall come:
they've caaed aa gowks fur blinks o blether
    baith deep and dumb.

In stately manses Haggismen
puhl sheeps' wames owre thir heids and then
descend beh greenie poles tae dens
    whaur desks await;
they raise thir stumpy Haggispens
    and smear on slates.

While maskless weemen keep ut edgy
an gee wir man a retro-wedgie –
remind us hoo his views got sketchy
    on burds and… beasts;
demand thir haggises be veggie
    and, glorious, feast.

And aa the waant-tae-bes are Robins
mair willin tae wark hard than Dobbin
and fuhl o antifreeze fae bobbin
    fur bacon rinds –
thir beaks, aa chipped, let slip thi sobbin
    of achin minds.

Thi anely time that Scots gets read
is when thi year lukes nearly dead –
    it seems tae need extremes;
when winterin leaves are lipped wi frost
and wolf-pack winds pursue the lost
    and ink, in deep freeze, dreams.
When Naichur jinks yir toon's defence
    and bursts yir comfort's net
wi snaw fitbaas, then tae thi tense
    come wurds thi waurm furget:

deep-layerin, like swearin,
    we dig oot attitudes;
wi stanzas come answers
    tae city pseuds and prudes.

Whit Burns wiz sayin tae Lapraik
wiz whit we are's eneuch tae make
a puckle lines that salve life's paiks:
    we need nae ticks
nor teachers' nods, nor critics' shakes –
    we're no *that* thick.

Ut's no that anely crambo goes
that jingles oot, jejunely, woes:
Burns claims he disnae ken whit's prose,
    whit's poetry,
but see hoo crafty his rhyme flows,
    and braid as Tay.

Whit Burns bethankit Davie fur
wiz freenship in thi dargin dirr:
when, pure ramfeezlet, thochts gae whirr,
    tae knock back gills
by ithers' ingles, bields fae smirr,
    can stave aff ills.

But here Eh sit wi midnicht's nip,
or leh doon whaur thi verses slip,
or rise tae brose and habbies' grip
    aa oan ma tod,
neglectin meh professorship,
    in the nemm o Gode!

Fur twenty fehv years – mair – Eh've trehd
tae scrieve in Scots and it's nae leh
Eh'm nae young billy – why deny
    Eh've ootlived Burns?
Fae Davie tae Lapraik we fleh
    wi nae returns.

Ootlived, but no ootwritten yet,
nae superbard, nor *Guardian* pet
nor whit maist fowk wad read;
tho fit fur (no sae) prehvut letters
wi a dictionair sae crossword-setters
    micht love me when Eh'm deid.
But whit Burns foond inben oor speak's
    a glede fur aa McSlackers:
gin Doric's heat is kin tae Greek
    Eh'll scrieve 'To a Moussaka.'
And thi ithers? Jist brithers
    and sisters eftir aa:
still-hopefu peers and hoped-fur feres –
    Eh think thi ink micht thaw…

I found myself being drawn towards Burns's epistles because of their blithe irreverence; something about Burns writing these almost-private letters, half-knowing they'd be read, spoke to me. Read by people who might well be gentry, or the learned folk he satirises, caught between envy and pity – rhymes to be overheard by those who didn't have to labour as he and his correspondents did, hard physical work in the cold.

    I liked both the wintriness and the exhaustion – the cold snap that astonished the south of England was fresh in my mind, as were the heaps of marking, etc. I was wading through. Not exactly a snowdrift, but it freezes the imagination. I also liked the irony that here was someone who may have learnt Scots in a Dundee tenement, but who had, despite much feckless ineptitude, ended up a professor, empathising with a man who mock-dismisses university education in favour of self-knowledge.

    The epistles have an edge I wanted to reflect by, if not quite biting the hand that commissioned me, certainly giving it a nip.

As the poem says, I and a few others have been writing in Scots for, euphemistically, a while, and as a result are accustomed to becoming 'interesting' around certain dates, while the rest of the year/decade Scots is consigned to its kennel of outmoded incomprehensibility. I wanted to say something about that incomprehension.

Burns's language is so filled with a liveliness of register, rhythm and vocabulary, I find I sometimes don't understand why people don't understand him – surely the sheer exuberance of that voice must knock everyone's poetry socks off. And then I remember we don't all own or choose to wear our poetry socks. Much of what Burns says, like much of what Shakespeare says, must now be assumed to be brilliant because people like me bang on about it. And surely nothing people like me are enthusiastic about can really be any good.

But one of the things I've always loved about Burns is his improvisational energy – when he says he's going to stay up all night and write the poem, you not only believe him, you want him to do exactly that, you want the ideas that come because he's put himself on the spot, and the immediacy and intimacy that comes with that, something that brings us back to what it is to write a letter.

No one writes letters anymore, or no one younger than fifty, but everyone has that moment when they catch themselves communicating full-tilt with someone else, in the excited knowledge that the ideas are just flowing, each from the previous. What Burns does, in such a masterful manner it's practically invisible, is give the impression he's dashing off a few such thoughts in two of the most intricate stanza forms Scots has, the Cherrie and the Slae, and the Standard Habbie.

Poetry at its best is always poised between absolute control and completely unpredictable freedom, between perfectly-cadenced utterance and the roughest turn of phrase, between the arcane image and the most everyday occurrence. It occurs when one of these turns into its opposite, or appears to – and this is what happens over and over as we eavesdrop on Burns anticipating a dram with Lapraik, or sharing a sly joke with Davie. I had no one equivalent to write to for my poem, so I thought of you.

W.N. HERBERT

Epistle to a Young Friend

I LANG hae thought, my youthfu' friend,
  A Something to have sent you,
Tho' it should serve nae other end
  Than just a kind memento;
But how the subject theme may gang,   *its message may turn out*
  Let time and chance determine;
Perhaps it may turn out a Sang;
  Perhaps, turn out a Sermon.

Ye'll try the world soon my lad,
  And ANDREW dear believe me,
Ye'll find mankind an unco squad,   *strange bunch*
  And muckle they may grieve ye: *greatly*
For care and trouble set your thought,
  Ev'n when your end's attained;
And a' your views may come to nought,
  Where ev'ry nerve is strained.

I'll no say, men are villains a';
  The real, harden'd wicked,
Wha hae nae check but *human law*,
  Are to a few restricked: *restricted*
But Och, mankind are unco weak,   *exceptionally*
  An' little to be trusted;
If *Self* the wavering balance shake,
  It's rarely right adjusted!

Yet they wha fa' in Fortune's strife,
  Their fate we should na censure,
For still th' *important end* of life,
  They equally may answer:
A man may hae an *honest heart*,
  Tho' Poortith hourly stare him;   *poverty*
A man may tak a neebor's part,   *neighbour's*
  Yet hae nae *cash* to spare him.

Ay free, aff han', your story tell,   *always freely, in an easy way*
  When wi' a bosom crony;
But still keep something to yoursel

Ye scarcely tell to ony.
Conceal yoursel as weel 's ye can
    Frae critical dissection;
But keek thro' ev'ry other man,   *cautiously glance*
    Wi' sharpen'd, sly inspection.

The *sacred lowe* o' weel plac'd love,   *holy flame*
    Luxuriantly indulge it;
But never tempt th' *illicit rove*,   *forbidden affair*
    Tho' naething should divulge it:
I wave the quantum o' the sin;   *portion, amount*
    The hazard of concealing;
But Och! it hardens *a' within*,
    And petrifies the feeling!

To catch Dame Fortune's golden smile,
    Assiduous wait upon her;
And gather gear by ev'ry wile,   *wealth and property*
    That's justify'd by Honor:
Not for to *hide* in it a *hedge*,
    Not for a *train-attendant*;
But for the glorious priviledge
    Of being *independant*.

The *fear o' Hell*'s a hangman's whip,
    To haud the wretch in order;   *hold*
But where ye feel your *Honor* grip,
    Let that ay be your border:
It's slightest touches, instant pause—
    Debar a' side-pretences;
And resolutely keep it's laws,
    Uncaring consequences.   *heedless of the consequences*

The great CREATOR to revere,
    Must sure become the *Creature*;
But still the preaching cant forbear:
    And ev'n the rigid feature:
Yet ne'er with Wits prophane to range,
    Be complaisance extended;
An *atheist-laugh* 's a poor exchange
    For *Deity offended*!

When ranting round in Pleasure's ring,
    Religion may be blinded;
Or if she gie a *random-fling*,   give
    It may be little minded;
But when on Life we're tempest-driven,
    A Conscience but a canker—   grumble
A correspondence fix'd wi' Heav'n,
    Is sure a noble *anchor*!

Adieu, dear, amiable Youth!
    Your *heart* can ne'er be wanting!
May Prudence, Fortitude and Truth
    Erect your brow undaunting!
In *ploughman phrase* 'God send you speed,'
    Still daily to grow wiser;
And may ye better reck the *rede*,   heed the advice
    Than ever did th' *Adviser*!

Robert Crawford

The Marble Quarry

For the second time in fifty years
I come to the Marble Quarry.
Last time, a boy, I came with my father.
Now I am here with my son.
Afternoon heat streams from the marble,
White light chipped from the earth.
At the island quarry's hoist and jetty
Underwater abandoned altars,
Veined slabs, shine through the waves.
We eye up shards among the scarred,
Discarded blocks. I tell my son
How my dad handed me a monumental
Offcut, heavy as an unfinished temple.
We scour what's left. I pick a piece
That fits my hand, and hand it to him
Gingerly. It fits his hand too.

W hen I saw that Burns's 'Epistle to a Young Friend'
was to be part of the contents of this book, I was
intrigued. Though its celebration of 'being *independant*' may glance
towards better known poems, this is not a Burns poem that would
rank among my favourites. Yet its theme and its balance between
openness and secrecy appeal to me, and I thought I had a poem
that might sit beside it – a few seats along the same pew.

The parent-child relationship had some interest for Burns,
who wrote about his own father and celebrated his household in 'The
Cotter's Saturday Night'. Whether or not she grew to like it, Burns
did address a poem to his first-born daughter, but, as far as we know,
he never addressed poems to any of his sons. In writing his 'Epistle to
a Young Friend' for his 'youthfu' friend' Andrew Hunter Aiken, son of
Burns's Ayr lawyer and supporter Robert Aiken, Burns came as close as
he ever did to writing a poem addressed from a father to a son. I find
this 1786 poem a little too pious, and suspect Burns (whose own life
was as complex as ever at the time) was preaching to himself when he
considered 'th' *illicit rove*'. The bit of the poem I like best are the lines
where he advises the youth to 'still keep something to yoursel/ Ye scarcely
tell to ony.' If this verse epistle is full of explicit advice-giving, it is also
about a subtler transmission of values from one generation to the next,
and it's powered by a wish to stay faithful to something handed down.

We're quite wary now about this sort of formal advice-
giving, and about ideas of inherited wisdom. Men may be more
awkward about these things than women. In my poem, conscious I
was approaching the age of fifty, I wanted to write very plainly and
openly about an experience I shared with my fourteen-year-old son,
but which also reminded me (and was patterned on) an experience I
had shared with my father when I was aged about fourteen. The poem
was written substantially in 2008 when we went for a long walk on the
island of Iona on a very hot day – but if the setting seems a bit more
Mediterranean and Classical, that's fine by me. It involves a moment
between my son and me, but also wider concerns of handing down,
passing on what matters. In some ways it's very open, but it's trying, too,
to communicate something not said, not fully spelled out. Sometimes
it's poetry's wish to bring together openness with a wish to smuggle
the unsayable that makes it matter. A poem is an open secret.

ROBERT CRAWFORD

Mary Morison

O Mary, at thy window be,
    It is the wish'd, the trysted hour;   *appointed*
Those smiles and glances let me see,
    That make the miser's treasure poor:
How blythely wad I bide the stoure,   *how happily would I bear the struggle*
    A weary slave frae sun to sun;
Could I the rich reward secure,
    The lovely Mary Morison!

Yestreen when to the trembling string   *last night*
    The dance gaed through the lighted ha',   *went*
To thee my fancy took its wing,
    I sat, but neither heard, nor saw:
Though this was fair, and that was braw,   *fine*
    And yon the toast of a' the town,   *that other one*
I sigh'd, and said amang them a',
    'Ye are na Mary Morison.'

O Mary, canst thou wreck his peace,
    Wha for thy sake wad gladly die!
Or canst thou break that heart of his,
    Whase only faute is loving thee!   *fault*
If love for love thou wilt na gie,   *will not give*
    At least be pity to me shown;
A thought ungentle canna be
    The thought o' Mary Morison.

Carol Ann Duffy

Sung

Now only words in a rhyme,
no more than a name
on a stone,
and that well overgrown—
MAR–   – ORIS—;

and wind though a ruined croft,
the door an appalled mouth,
the window's eye put out;

hours and wishes and trysts
less than the shadows of clouds on grass,
ghosts that did dance, did dance...

and those who would gladly die for love lang deid-
a skull for a bonnie head-
and love itself a metaphor, rose, red.

M ost of my childhood was spent in England

where my family had moved from Glasgow. I had an Irish mother who'd grown up in Scotland and a Scottish father whose grandparents were Irish – so I felt an affinity with all three countries. It wasn't, at all, a bookish house and the only poet who was ever quoted was Robert Burns – not only at Hogmanay, but when someone saw a mouse (Wee sleeket , cowran tim'rous *beastie*) or got above themselves (O wad some Pow'r the giftie gie us/ *To see oursels as others see us!*). My father, who fancied himself – and this was open to debate – as a terrific singer, would occasionally throw in a Burns song along with the Rat Pack Medley, 'My Way' and 'Flower of Scotland'. So Burns was the first poet I knew by name and seemed forever linked to our emigration from Scotland. Poetry became important to me quite early – I was lucky with my teachers and had a small but wonderful local library run by a kindly, first-name terms, librarian – and since my adolescence Burns, for me, has been one of the greatest of all love poets. In fact, the older I get, the greater his love poems seem – simple, memorable, lyrical, true and deeply human. 'Mary Morison' has always been my favourite, especially since I was once lucky enough to have it recited to me by another late, great Scots poet, Norman MacCaig, over a few whiskies after a poetry reading together. I loved the way Burns named the woman in the poem and by doing so made her unique, the only one, the sole object of his passion. His voice is almost in our ear when we read this. Almost living. Here, my response to the poem is a fractured sonnet which is an elegy for dead lovers and which follows my instinct that, like Yeats after him, Burns would have rather had the girl than written the poem. The last line echoes another much-loved Burns love poem and gives him, rightly, the last word.

CAROL ANN DUFFY

A red red Rose

O MY Luve 's like a red, red rose,
  That 's newly sprung in June;
O my Luve 's like the melodie
  That 's sweetly play'd in tune.—

As fair art thou, my bonie lass,
  So deep in luve am I;
And I will love thee still, my Dear,
  Till a' the seas gang dry.—

Till a' the seas gang dry, my Dear,
  And the rocks melt wi' the sun:
I will love thee still, my Dear,
  While the sands o' life shall run.—

And fare thee weel, my only Luve!
  And fare thee weel, a while!
And I will come again, my Luve,
  Tho' it were ten thousand mile!

Matthew Fitt

Rose

Ye hink ah'm like a reid, reid whit?
You dinna hae a scoob!
And whit dae you ken aboot melodie?
Dae ye hink ah'm a tube?

And whit's aw this aboot seas gaun dry
When we're hauf droont in your slavers?
It's your brain must be meltit, pal,
Comin oot wi aw this havers.

And sauns o life? It's ower the tap.
Ye'll dae yirsel a mischief.
Ten thoosand mile? Aye, on ye go.
Fare thee weel… richt ower the first cliff.

Ye're aff? Hing on, ah'll chum ye doon
This road a bit, see jist whaur it goes.
Naw, wait the noo, ma glaikit doo –
Did ye no ken ye had me at 'rose'?

Ye cannae appreciate the poetry o Robert Burns until ye believe in his language. Ye dinnae hae tae be fluent in it or talk it aw the time but ye dae hae tae ken twa things: thing wan – it's cawed Scots; thing twa – it's no cawed 'slang'. Onybody that reckons Burns's language is 'slang' and no Scots needs tae awa and dook their heid in the River Doon.

I waled 'A red red Rose' because I feel Burns wantit this poem (it's a sang as weel) tae hae mair tae it than jist 'I love ye, I think ye're great, I'll love ye forever and ever, sae I wull.'

Burns wrote a guid wheen love poems but I've aye been intrigued by the speaker in this yin. Some fowk claim the speaker is Burns himsel but it could easy be ony laddie, lassie, man or wumman tellin anither person (or thing) they love them. I've aften thocht this speaker is a mair complex character than meets the ee.

He/she comes oot wi bonnie stottin big-hertit sentiments that wid mak maist folk weak at the hurdies. 'Til aw the seas gang dry', they say. Impressive stuff because seas dinnae gang dry owernicht. Then the speaker says, 'I'll love ye tae the rocks melt wi the sun', an even langer time. And then he/she says their love's gonnae last 'while the sands o life shall run' – basically until awbody on the planet's deid.

Then it's no hoo lang but hoo faur: no jist roond the corner or tae the chipper and back but ten thoosand miles which if ye did that walkin fae George Square in Glesga ye wid probably end up at the Sydney Opera Hoose in Australia. It micht weel be the speaker's love is that muckle that they hae tae say muckle things tae match. (There's a name for that: it's cawed 'hyperbole'.)

But although the speaker is giein it plenty aboot roses and seas dryin oot, I suspect it could be the ither person is jist no interested. Mibbe the listener doesnae want tae ken, thinks the speaker is a bit hackit and mingin and wid raither run ten thoosand miles in the ither direction. Or mibbe the listener is secretly pure lappin up aw the beautiful similes and gallus hyperbole and is jist pretendin no tae be impressed hopin the speaker will come up wi mair statements o their love, each yin mair muckle and amazin than the last.

Write a monologue fae the view-point o a person like the speaker in 'A red red Rose'. Ye could hae some fun as they exaggerate hoo great their love is, or mibbe they're no awfie guid at expressin their love and get teased a little (or a lot) by the ither person. Ye could write fae the ither person's point o view as weel like in the poem I've written here. Or ye could hae baith voices gaun at it thegither in a short story or a playscript.

Whitever ye dae, try writin in Scots. There's nae better wey tae understand the poetry and sangs o Robert Burns than tae read and write in his and your ain tongue.

MATTHEW FITT

John Anderson my Jo

JOHN Anderson my jo, John,   *love, sweetheart*
    When we were first acquent;   *acquainted*
Your locks were like the raven,
    Your bony brow was brent;   *smooth, unwrinkled*
But now your brow is beld, John,   *bald*
    Your locks are like the snaw;
But blessings on your frosty pow,   *head*
    John Anderson my Jo.

John Anderson my jo, John,
    We clamb the hill the gither;   *together*
And mony a canty day, John,   *happy, jolly*
    We've had wi' ane anither:
Now we maun totter down, John,   *must*
    And hand in hand we'll go;
And sleep the gither at the foot,
    John Anderson my Jo.

Jackie Kay

Fiere

If ye went tae the tapmost hill, Fiere
Whaur we used tae clamb as girls,
Ye'd see the snow the day, Fiere,
Settling on the hills.
You'd mind o' anither day, mibbe,
We ran doon the hill in the snow,
Sliding and singing oor way tae the foot,
Lassies laughing thegither – how braw.
The years slipping awa; oot in the weather.

And noo we're suddenly auld, Fiere,
Oor friendship's ne'er been weary.
We've aye seen the wurld differently.
Whaur would I hae been weyoot my jo,
My fiere, my fiercy, my dearie O?
Oor hair micht be silver noo,
Oor walk a wee bit doddery,
But we've had a whirl and a blast, girl,
Thru' the cauld blast winter, thru spring, summer.

O'er a lifetime, my fiere, my bonnie lassie,
I'd defend you – you, me; blithe and blatter,
Here we gang doon the hill, nae matter,
Past the bracken, bothy, bonny braes, barley.
Oot by the roaring Sea, still havin a blether.
We who loved sincerely; we who loved sae fiercely.
The snow ne'er looked sae barrie,
Nor the winter trees sae pretty.
C'mon, c'mon my dearie – tak my hand, my fiere!

A good friend of my parents, Anna Ashton, used to sing 'John Anderson my Jo' beautifully in my house where sing-songs were often held when I was a wee girl. I loved that song in particular. I liked picturing the couple, the way they went from young to old, with their love still intact. 'Now we maun totter down John', is obviously, now that I'm an adult, about them dying, but I never realised that at the time. I just found it moving, them going down the hill hand in hand.

'John Anderson, my Jo' captures a whole life in the shortest stanzas; the length of the stanzas makes you think about the brevity of life, the possible comfort of dying together, 'And sleep thegither at the foot'. Short poems are about the only form that can manage to span a lifetime so beautifully. John Anderson changes from having locks like the raven to locks like the snow.

I have not attempted two short stanzas because I didn't think I could pull that off. I decided to take the idea of friendship – 'jo' is an old Scots word for friend – and write about a lifelong friendship between two excited girls who become two old women. (Their hair colour also changes!) 'Fiere' is also an old word for friend, to be found in 'Auld Lang Syne', 'And there's a hand my trusty *fiere*'. I've used Fiere because it looks like fierce – the two friends in my poem are *fierce friends*: they'd defend each other to the hilt. It's snowing in the poem because John's locks are like the snow, and also because it was snowing outside my study window when I wrote it, the heaviest snowfall for eighteen years! The last line 'tak my hand' I wanted to echo 'Auld Lang Syne'. I liked the idea of attempting to address more than one poem, so there's also a little echo from 'Ae Fond Kiss' in there too. I didn't want to exactly copy the original but more to nod to it, and to try and write a poem that showed a love of Burns in general. (I'd have loved trying to fit a mouse, a louse, a tailless horse, a haggis, a Willy Wastle and a Holy Willie all into the one poem – but that seemed a bit crazy!)

I wanted to write a poem about friendship and to celebrate friendship. So many poems celebrate romantic love, and not so many celebrate the love for a trusty friend. The friend in this poem is real, a true fierce friend. I've kept the friend without a name in the poem so that hopefully she could remind the reader of the reader's friends. In my poem, I'm also imagining the friendship getting old since my hair ain't silver yet!

JACKIE KAY

Robert Bruce's March to Bannockburn (Scots wha hae)

SCOTS, wha hae wi' WALLACE bled,   who have
Scots, wham BRUCE has aften led,   whom
Welcome to your gory bed,—
     Or to victorie.—

Now 's the day, and now 's the hour;
See the front o' battle lour;   threaten
See approach proud EDWARD's power,
     Chains and Slaverie.—

Wha will be a traitor-knave?
Wha can fill a coward's grave?
Wha sae base as be a Slave?
     —Let him turn and flie:—

Wha for SCOTLAND's king and law,
Freedom's sword will strongly draw,
FREE-MAN stand, or FREE-MAN fa',
     Let him follow me.—

By Oppression's woes and pains!
By your Sons in servile chains!
We will drain our dearest veins,
     But they *shall* be free!

Lay the proud Usurpers low!
Tyrants fall in every foe!
LIBERTY's in every blow!
     Let us DO—OR DIE!!!

Janet Paisley

Aw Jock Tamson's

Moonrise, an maudlin in the mirk,
we coorie in, hoose selt, hame hawked,
oor labour thirled tae yesterday,
the morra pawned fur brick-a-brack.

Thieves tout the mercat, flashin cash
in credit caird tricks yince cried tick.
Gowks gawp. It's easy money. Hauns
dip threidbare pooches skint by lees;

yin cat feeds fat, an hunners sterve.
Dunderheids, we bocht intae grief,
gied up sense fur greed, furgoat brass
barters work, its worth inventit.

A dreich rain faws oan rentit roofs.
We pey tae drain the run-aff, pey
again tae pipe it back. Nae debt
is gain. If lochs fill, mountains droon.

Yit bairns sleep an dream, fit tae bigg
a warld whaur love gies shelter, breid
daily, care redds up, prood tae bide
an fecht whaur fowk cry foul at cheats:

nae man worth mair. It's wha we are.
Tak tent. Waukened, sleeves rowed up,
drookit, set tae work, a new stert.
Day breks, mornin sun ay rises.

Some instinct chose 'Scots wha hae' for me. It's a dramatised, monologue poem. One character – Robert the Bruce – speaks in a set situation – before the Battle of Bannockburn. I write many dramatic monologues. So did Burns. This one borrows from the 1320 Declaration of Arbroath, when Bruce was king. It's inspiring. Freedom, it says, is more valuable than life, and so it's worth dying for.

That seems like a big choice to make. I made it once. There was no army to fight, just a bully. The weapon I needed was courage – the courage to say no, to run away, and to tell the people who could help me and my children. It was frightening. I expected to die. But I chose to be free for a short time, if that's how it turned out, rather than be bullied again. As soon as that choice was made, the bully had lost, whatever he did.

It's a big word, freedom – a concept. It means different things to people. Burns was writing about national freedom. The energy of his language, and how he uses it, is also inspiring. The words, when strung together, had to cause the kind of bravery that can run towards sharp spears and swords. These hurt. The poet had to create feelings strong enough to overcome common sense, which would tell most folk to run the other way.

To write my response, everything we need to fight against in Scotland today swirled round in my head, all jumbled up. I expected to write a monologue, and a funny one – lines for it are still living in my head. Don't, I told myself, don't write about politics. Do not even think of tackling the credit crunch. But the bit of my brain that writes poetry doesn't listen to the sensible part that gets me safely across the road.

Using the idea of freedom, money has become a thug. It dictates our lives. Some folk have far too much, some have far too little. Yet people invented it to make life easier, not harder. So, when my poem was ready to be written, that's what it was about. There is no character speaking. The poem has its own voice. It talks about credit, about borrowing. It says something like: if we spend our income before we earn it, we enslave ourselves.

I hope it reminds us that, when any one of us can act as a greedy individual, then we're all poor in the ways that matter. We're all responsible if our family, group, society, and world, suffers as many people go without. Thousands become poor so that a few can have more than they need. Is that riches? We've passed laws to make people tolerant, and we can make laws which create compassion. Money is a tool, not a weapon. It will work how we make it work. I'm too old to have much future, so it's up to you. Sorry it's not funny.

JANET PAISLEY

Holy Willie's Prayer

And send the Godly in a pet to pray—

Pope

O Thou that in the heavens does dwell!
Wha, as it pleases best thysel,
Sends ane to heaven and ten to h–ll,
      A' for thy glory!
And no for ony gude or ill
      They've done before thee.—

I bless and praise thy matchless might,
When thousands thou has left in night,
That I am here before thy sight,
      For gifts and grace,
A burning and a shining light
      To a' this place.—

What was I, or my generation,
That I should get such exaltation?
I, wha deserv'd most just damnation,
      For broken laws
Sax thousand years ere my creation,
      Thro' Adam's cause!

before my conception

When from my mother's womb I fell,
Thou might hae plunged me deep in hell,
To gnash my gooms, and weep, and wail,
      In burning lakes,
Where damned devils roar and yell
      Chain'd to their stakes.—

Yet I am here, a chosen sample,
To shew thy grace is great and ample:
I'm here, a pillar o' thy temple
      Strong as a rock,
A guide, a ruler and example
      To a' thy flock.—

[O L—d thou kens what zeal I bear,
When drinkers drink, and swearers swear,
And singin' there, and dancin' here,
    Wi' great an' sma';
For I am keepet by the thy fear,
    Free frae them a'.—]

But yet—O L—d—confess I must—
At times I'm fash'd wi' fleshly lust;   *tormented, troubled*
And sometimes too, in warldly trust   *worldly thoughts, habits*
    Vile Self gets in;
But thou remembers we are dust,
    Defil'd wi' sin.—

O L—d—yestreen—thou kens—wi' Meg— *last night; you know*
Thy pardon I sincerely beg!
O may 't ne'er be a living plague,
    To my dishonor!
And I'll ne'er lift a lawless leg
    Again upon her.—

Besides, I farther maun avow,   *must admit*
Wi' Leezie's lass, three times—I trow— *admit*
But L—d, that friday I was fou   *drunk*
    When I cam near her;
Or else, thou kens, thy servant true
    Wad never steer her.— *bother*

Maybe thou lets this fleshy thorn
Buffet thy servant e'en and morn,
Lest he o'er proud and high should turn,
    That he 's sae gifted;
If sae, thy hand maun e'en be borne *must even*
    Untill thou lift it.—

L—d bless thy Chosen in this place,
For here thou has a chosen race:
But G—d, confound their stubborn face,
    And blast their name,
Wha bring thy rulers to disgrace
    And open shame.—

L—d mind Gaun Hamilton's deserts!
He drinks, and swears, and plays at cartes,   cards
Yet has sae mony taking arts
    Wi' Great and Sma',
Frae G—d's ain priest the people's hearts
    He steals awa.—

And when we chasten'd him therefore,
Thou kens how he bred sic a splore,   such an uproar
And set the warld in a roar
    O' laughin at us:
Curse thou his basket and his store,
    Kail and potatoes.—   kind of cabbage

L—d hear my earnest cry and prayer
Against that Presbytry of Ayr!
Thy strong right hand, L—d, make it bare
    Upon their heads!
L—d visit them, and dinna spare,
    For their misdeeds!

O L—d my G—d, that glib-tongu'd Aiken!
My very heart and flesh are quaking
To think how I sat, sweating, shaking,
    And p—ss'd wi' dread,
While Auld wi' hingin lip gaed sneaking
    And hid his head!

L—d, in thy day o' vengeance try him!
L—d visit him that did employ him!
And pass not in thy mercy by them,
        Nor hear their prayer;
But for thy people's sake destroy them,
        And dinna spare!

But L—d, remember me and mine
Wi' mercies temporal and divine!
That I for grace and gear may shine,
        Excell'd by nane!
And a' the glory shall be thine!
        Amen! Amen!

Rab Wilson

Holy Gordon's Prayer

O Lord my God, forgie this swither,
pray hear thy servant in his dither.
Should ah bide here? or cross the river –
        braid Rubicon –
(for hum an haw dis not luik cliver)
        or sodger oan?

Kings 18:21

Thou minds ah 'bottled it' aince afore,
when Cameron let oot sic a sploar –
Thou kens there's nocht that he'd like more,
than an election –
faa him an aa his Tory corps,
        fowks' fell rejection!

Numbers 22:6

Shair Lord, thaim wi the mense tae see,
the path that you hae guidit me,   *Exodus 3:8*
wid ne'er dout that ma destiny,
                              is mappit oot!
Keep mind, the warld wis sauved by me,
                              withooten dout!

Your aid ah kent as foes ah trod oan,
As oligarchs felled taintit Osborne.
They felt ma wrath, ah strapt your sword oan,   *Leviticus 26:7*
                              tae wreak thaim ill,
But thou kens ah'm no 'Flash' – juist Gordon,
                              Sent at your will.

Mind, it's no juist the Opposeetion,
that poses threits tae ma poseetion,
Blunkett, Clarke, an in addeetion,
                              young Miliband,
Cuid you no send *thaim* tae perdeetion –
                              an rax yer haund?   *Exodus 15:6*

But, ah'm the man that ye hae chosen,   *1 Samuel 10:24*
Dreepin wi benison o unction
Your haund ah saw in Blair's expulsion,   *Leviticus 16:10*
                              Tae the desert air,
Ah'd ne'er hae taen back Mandelson,
                              Hud ah no bin shair.

Blair! Oan his throne! That wis *ma* chair!   *1 Kings 1:13*
Nou dinnae think ah'm bein unfair,
Lord mind, 'twis you that kept him there,
                              fir aa thae years,
while thon Cherie gaed smirkin, shair,
                              wi snipes an sneers.

While nou? He thinks tae get tae Heivin?
Ye'll mind, that war wis *his* deceesion!
Thae tens o thoosans slain – *his* veesion –   *1 Samuel 18:7*
                              nane doun ti me –
Ah pleadit wi him, '*Tone, see reason…*'
                              He'd een tae see.   *Deuteronomy 21:7*

It's bin a lang road frae Kirkcaldy;
fir years ah languisht – his 'dogsbody',
while he gaed roond the warld tae toady,
        a braizent scrounger! –   *John 9:8*
tae Bush, Cliff Richard, Berlusconi –
        the beggin cadger!

Ma bairntid, aye; curst parsimony,
Thon wis nae land o milk an honey.   *Exodus 3:8*
Auld John wid aiblins think it funny,
        Ah've foun the key,
Tae sairve baith maisters – God an Money,   *Matthew 6:24*
        in like degree.

An did the fowk gie me their thanks   *1 Chronicles 29:13*
fir bailin oot their Scottish banks?
Ah micht bin better sendin tanks,
        tae quell their bleatin.
An wha's tae blame, Lord? Aye, the Yanks!
        Tae *thaim* gang greetin!

Economy wis stupit, thanks –
They're blamin me, gaun doun the stanks,   *2 Samuel 22:24*
but Madoff wi his Ponzi pranks
        wis ill tae trust:
no ma faut that the British banks
        gaed boom, syne bust!

Thae billions aff fowks' 'Pensions Scheme',
wis mine bi richts, tae fund ma dream!
Sae whit, gin ah straikt aff some cream,   *Job 29:6*
        fir odd 'Fat-Cats'?
It's juist a fact, Lord: Mammon's stream,
        aye droons some rats!

Ma pure an flawless disposeetion,   *Job 11:4*
Sees me steer clear o aa corruption,
Ma jaunts wi Geoffrey Robinson,
                    tae fitba matches,
Wis sanctiont tae enhance relations –
                    read the Dispatches!

Mind, Rome fair bates 'Stark's Park' Lord, whiles,
'Raith Rovers' native domicile,
Wha lead the 'Irn Bru' league wi style!
                    Nae feet o clay!   *Daniel 2:33*
Ah fervent pray ye'll oan thaim smile,   *Job 29:24*
                    Hame or Away!

But here: ah'm gaun 'aff-message' Lord.
Thou kens they'r blissed that hears thy Wurd.   *Numbers 24:4*
No leeterally! – thon's absurd!
                    Hou Bush gaed oan!
(Nae rael surprise that thon man heard
                    Ye oan his phone!)

Shuid ah announce a snap election,
in this, the kintra's warst recession?
It wid be nice Lord, an Ascension –
                    Wi ma ain Mandate!
Ah'm fed up wi the allegation –
                    'Wha hesitates is baet.'   *Job 30:10*

Mak the Juidgement o ma story;
'Gorgeous Gordo pips the Tory!'
Juist think o whit tabloid furore
                    Gart Dave resign?
Ye hae ma wurd Lord, aa the Glory
                    Shall be Thine!   *I Chronicles 16:8*

Amen!

W hen ah wis approached bi the Scottish Poetry
Library tae play a pairt in their ongauns tae re-write/re-imagine
ane o Burns's greatest warks (we wir gien a leet o the poems we culd
chuise frae, ah said ah wid be happy tae tackle white'er wis left eftir the
ither makars hud made their walin! Hence ah wis the yin left wi 'Holy
Willie's Prayer'!). It wis wi some sense o trepidation that ah approacht
this michtiest an maist famous o the Bard's satires.

Ah think it's kindae deeficult fir fowks leevin in this secular
age tae get their heids roond the importance that releegion played in
society, an the pouer it still exertit, at the time o Burns. Gin he'd wrote
this piece a hunner year earlier there's nae dout he wid hae bin hung fir
sic blasphemy. Perhaps, in a wey, 'Holy Willie' is an exaumpil o hou faur
tolerance an common sense hud advanced in Scotland throu the teachins
o the Enlichtenment?

Fir masel, ah am an atheist, sae tacklin this wark hud addit
problems! But ah am alsae siccar in masel in screivin Scots an, lik Burns
hissel, ah'm no averse tae 'writin fir fun', an ah enjoy writin topical
poleetical satire nou an agane. Sae, in a wey, this ploy wis 'Caviar to the
General'!

'Holy Willie', William Fisher (1737-1809), wis a native o
Mauchline, an kirk elder, wha invoked Burns's ire, an satirical wrath,
fir steerin up a releegious '*coort-case*' anent Burns's guid frien Gavin
Hamilton. In Janwar 1785 the '*Moderate*' Presbytery o Ayr ordert the
erasure o the Mauchline kirk session meenits anent Hamilton; the case
went tae appeal, but Hamilton won an wis gien a certificate lowsin him
frae ony ecclesiastical censure. Ye can imagine the anger an indignation o
Willie Fisher at these ongauns, an thus the imagined prayer that the self-
richteous Willie declaims tae heivin.

'Holy Willie's Prayer' wis written they reck directly eftir anither o ane o Burns's great releegious satires, 'The Holy Tulzie', sae Burns wid hae bin oan a bit o a roll writin stuff that involved the direct uise o biblical references. Burns wid hae bin brocht up wi a deep knowledge o the Bible an it wid hae bin saicent nature fir him tae quote frae it when'er the need arose. Gin ony o the readers o this want tae fuin oot mair anent Burns's poem, or the events surroundin its creatioun, then ah strangly encourage thaim tae read James Mckay's influential *Burns; a Biography of Robert Burns*, and alsae tae consult the magisterial three volume edeetion *The Poems and Songs of Robert Burns* bi James Kinsley – ye wull not be disapyntit!

But tae oor tale! Wha did ah chuise fir ma modren 'Holy Willie'? weel, unfortunately Tony Blair is nou history, an onywey, ah'd bin bate tae him bi Tony Harrison wha hus aareadies writ 'Holy Tony's Prayer' – albeit he anely gied Blair a drubbin in rhyming doggerel couplets, while the subject o ma tirade gets the full 'Staundart Habbie' (Burns's regular poetic metre) treatment! Ma subject hud tae be thon kenspeckle Scotsman, hailin frae Kirkcaldy, skeelie politeecian, son o the manse, an oor current Prime Meenister, Gordon Brown.

As wi Burns's version ah hae consultit the Bible tae try an ensure that 'Holy Gordon' is gien aa due respect anent its poetic pedigree. Readers may consult the 'guid buik' at their leesure tae fuin an conseider the exact quotations applied an cited. At the end o the day this lichtweicht squib o mine cams naewhaurs near the genius o Burns's satire – sic ploys as this wull generally ah'm thinkin produce anely technically correct, tho aiblins heirtfelt, tributes tae the man. Gin it maks ye lauch, think or smile tho, it wull hae achieved somethin.

RAB WILSON

Address of Beelzebub

Long Life, My lord, an' health be yours,
Unskaith'd by hunger'd Highlan Boors!   *unharmed*
Lord grant, nae duddie, desp'rate beggar,   *ragged*
Wi' durk, claymore, or rusty trigger
May twin auld Scotland o' a life,
She likes—as butchers like a knife!

Faith, you and Applecross were right
To keep the highlan hounds in sight!
I doubt na! they wad bid nae better   *I don't doubt that they would do nothing better*
Than let them ance out owre the water;
Then up amang thae lakes an' seas   *those*
They'll mak what rules an' laws they please.

Some daring Hancocke, or a Frankline,
May set their highlan bluid a ranklin;
Some Washington again may head them,
Or some Montgomery, fearless, lead them;
Till, God knows what may be effected,
When by such heads an' hearts directed:
Poor, dunghill sons of dirt an' mire,
May to Patrician rights aspire;
Nae sage North, now, nor sager Sackville,
To watch an' premier owre the pack vile!   *lord it over*
An' whare will ye get Howes an' Clintons
To bring them to a right repentance,
To cowe the rebel generation,   *scare, control*
An' save the honor o' the Nation?
They! an' be d—mn'd! what right hae they
To Meat, or Sleep, or light o' day,
Far less to riches, pow'r, or freedom,
But what your lordships please to gie them?

But hear me, my lord! Glengary hear!
Your hand's owre light on them, I fear: *over easy*
Your factors, greives, trustees an' bailies,
I canna say but they do gailies;   *I can't say but they do well enough*

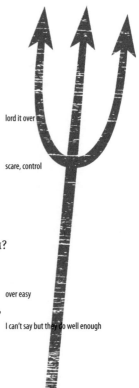

They lay aside a' tender mercies
An' tirl the HALLIONS to the BIRSIES;   strip the idlers to the skin
Yet, while they're only poin'd, and herriet,   plundered and robbed, harried
They'll keep their stubborn Highlan spirit.
But smash them! crush them a' to spails!   pieces
An' rot the DYVORS i' the JAILS!   debtors
The young dogs, swinge them to the labour,   whip
Let WARK an' HUNGER mak them sober!   work
The HIZZIES, if they're oughtlins fausont,   girls; in any way good looking
Let them in DRURY LANE be lesson'd!   let them be taught in Drury Lane i.e. become prostitutes
An' if the wives, an' dirty brats,
Come thiggan at your doors an' yets,   begging; gates
Flaffan wi' duds, an' grey wi' beese,   flapping with rags and grey with vermin
Frightan awa your deucks an' geese;   ducks
Get out a HORSE-WHIP, or a JOWLER,   bulldog
The langest thong, the fiercest growler,
An' gar the tatter'd gipseys pack   make
Wi' a' their bastarts on their back!

Go on, my lord! I lang to meet you
An' in my HOUSE AT HAME to greet you;   i.e. in Hell
Wi' COMMON LORDS ye shanna mingle,   shall not
The benmost newk, beside the ingle   innermost corner beside the fire
At my right hand, assign'd your seat
'Tween HEROD'S hip, an' POLYCRATE;
Or, if ye on your station tarrow,   doubt, hesitate
Between ALMAGRO and PIZARRO;
A seat, I'm sure ye're weel deservin 't;
An' till ye come—your humble servant

BEELZEBUB.

HELL 1st June Anno Mundi 5790

James Robertson

Beelzebub Resurfaces

A girnin, greitin deil wis I –
I wis auld, and feelin aulder.
Syne the heatin system burst in Hell:
It wis cauld – and gettin caulder.

When the fires were doun tae reek and ash,
And the cauldrons fou o ice,
And imps and bogles hunkered roond
Like cowrin, chitterin mice,

And the wretched deid were truly deid,
And had nae pain left tae thole –
I kent that it wis time tae leave
Yon dreich and dowie hole.

I trauchled up the auld stane stair,
Unsnecked the rousty yett,
And hard upon the stoury grund
Ma clootie fit I set.

The Earth wis yince a paradise –
It wis bonnie, bricht and braw,
And a sulky soor-mooth like masel
It didna please at aw.

But noo I fund a different scene,
That gart ma spirits lowp,
For man had made his paradise
A stinkin, scabbit cowp.

The land wis deid, the oceans deid,
The fush and wild beasts gane,
The rainforests were hackit doun,
And the rain wis acid rain;

Deserts had smoored the green fields ower,
The ice-caps were snaw-bree,
Floods had drouned the straths and glens,
And wild winds whipped the sea.

Fires bleezed that made aw Hell's fires seem
Mere skinkles in the nicht;
And, in their bonnie, beekin lowe,
O whit a glorious sicht!

God's craitur fechtin wi himsel
For ile and land and food,
For widd and water, graith and gear,
And – best o aw – for God;

Men busy killin ither men
Wi guns and bombs and tanks,
And slauchterin bairns and weemin tae –
And the deid piled up in ranks.

I minded whit I'd read langsyne
And clapped ma hauns wi glee,
For whit I saw looked awfie like
A Judgment Day tae me.

Sae aw ye princes, presidents
And ither heids o state,
Herrie and fyle, oppress, invade,
And dinna be ower blate.

And aw ye haly terrorists,
Be bauld and fou o faith,
And whaur ye ding doun tyranny
Raise misery and daith.

I am a stranger faur frae hame,
But I fairly like yer style,
Sae dinna mind me sittin here –
I dout I'll bide a while.

A girnin, greitin deil wis I –
A sair-faced auld doom-monger.
But noo I'm happy, and whit's mair –
I believe I'm gettin younger!

Burns's 'Address of Beelzebub' is a brilliant piece of invective against the abuse of power, in which he uses heavy irony to make his point. Burns wrote it in 1786, when he himself was on the verge of emigrating to Jamaica, but – perhaps because it was too risky to criticise a powerful man like the Earl of Breadalbane in print – it was not actually published till 1818, long after Burns's death. By that date the Highland Clearances were in full progress, but in 1786 they were in their very early stages, and in fact the poem attacks landowners for trying to *prevent* hundreds of poverty-stricken people leaving for a new life of liberty in Canada. The wealthy landowners living in London who composed the Highland Society, were actually raising money to send to their tenants so that they would stay in their homeland (and continue paying rent), but in Burns's view this charity was not only too little, too late, it was also a deliberate disincentive to the Highlanders to emigrate and make a better life for themselves.

Beelzebub, 'the prince of devils' according to St Matthew's Gospel (ch.12, v. 24), is second only to Satan in devil seniority. Adopting Beelzebub's voice, Burns praises the Earl of Breadalbane for keeping the 'Highland boors' under subjection, and exhorts him to be even harsher on them and break their spirits, sending the men to jail for their debts and the young women to Drury Lane in

London, where they can learn to make a living from prostitution.
If mothers and children come begging at the door, Beelzebub
advises, set the dogs on them. Meanwhile, he'll keep a seat in Hell
for the Earl next to some of the worst villains of ancient times.

      I wanted to write a poem that was as ferocious as Burns's,
and my preferred targets were those industrialists and politicians willing
to destroy unspoilt parts of the earth like Alaska and the Antarctic
in pursuit of mineral wealth. Beelzebub would surely approve of the
ruination of the planet for short-term gain. I thought I'd stick to the
same metre and rhyme-scheme that Burns uses in his poem, but
when I tried to put this plan into action it didn't work, and I ended
up with a few lines that were merely a pastiche of the original.

      My second idea was to aim at a wider target, and not to follow
Burns's format too strictly. It occurred to me that Beelzebub and his devil
colleagues would probably be completely reckless in their use of energy
in Hell, and this led me to speculate that when the fuel ran out *he* would
emigrate to somewhere warmer. I used a ballad form to describe what he
discovers when he ventures onto the surface of the Earth. The mayhem
and devastation suit him well: he has, in effect, found his own paradise – a
man-made Hell where he will be quite happy to watch humans behaving
abominably not just to the planet but to each other. It's a depressing
picture of the condition of the world but Beelzebub, at least, finds it
entertaining, and I hope that his attitude and use of language inject a little
humour, on the basis that if you didn't laugh, you would have to greit.

JAMES ROBERTSON

Tam o' Shanter. A Tale

WHEN chapman billies leave the street,	pedlar billies
And drouthy neebors, neebors meet,	thirsty
As market-days are wearing late,	
An' folk begin to tak the gate;	take the road
While we sit bousing at the nappy,	drinking ale
And getting fou and unco' happy,	drunk; very
We think na on the lang Scots miles,	don't think
The mosses, waters, slaps and styles,	bogs; gaps in walls and fences
That lie between us and our hame,	
Whare sits our sulky sullen dame,	
Gathering her brows like gathering storm,	
Nursing her wrath to keep it warm.	

This truth fand honest *Tam o' Shanter*,	found
As he frae Ayr ae night did canter,	one
(Auld Ayr, wham ne'er a town surpasses,	
For honest men and bonny lasses.)	

O *Tam*! hadst thou but been sae wise,	
As ta'en thy ain wife *Kate*'s advice!	as to have taken
She tauld thee weel thou was a skellum,	told; rascal
A blethering, blustering, drunken blellum;	boaster
That frae November till October,	
Ae market-day thou was nae sober;	one

That ilka melder, wi' the miller, *every meal-gathering*
Thou sat as lang as thou had siller; *money*
That every naig was ca'd a shoe on, *horse; shoed*
The smith and thee gat roaring fou on;
That at the L—d's house, even on Sunday,
Thou drank wi' Kirkton Jean till Monday.
She prophesied that late or soon,
Thou would be found deep drown'd in Doon;
Or catch'd wi' warlocks in the mirk, *wizards; darkness*
By *Alloway's* auld haunted kirk.

   Ah, gentle dames! it gars me greet, *makes me weep*
To think how mony counsels sweet,
How mony lengthen'd sage advices,
The husband frae the wife despises!

   But to our tale: Ae market-night,
Tam had got planted unco right; *exceptionally well, comfortably*
Fast by an ingle, bleezing finely, *fireside*
Wi' reaming swats, that drank divinely; *foaming ale*
And at his elbow, Souter *Johnny*, *cobbler*
His ancient, trusty, drouthy crony; *thirsty friend*
Tam lo'ed him like a vera brither;
They had been fou for weeks thegither. *together*
The night drave on wi' sangs and clatter; *passed swiftly*
And ay the ale was growing better: *always*
The landlady and *Tam* grew gracious,
Wi' favours, secret, sweet, and precious:
The Souter tauld his queerest stories;
The landlord's laugh was ready chorus:
The storm without might rair and rustle, *outside; roar*
Tam did na mind the storm a whistle.

   Care, mad to see a man sae happy,
E'en drown'd himsel amang the nappy: *amidst the ale*
As bees flee hame wi' lades o' treasure, *loads*
The minutes wing'd their way wi' pleasure;
Kings may be blest, but *Tam* was glorious,
O'er a' the ills o' life victorious!

But pleasures are like poppies spread,
You seize the flower, its bloom is shed;
Or like the snow falls in the river,
A moment white—then melts for ever;
Or like the borealis race,
That flit ere you can point their place;
Or like the rainbow's lovely form
Evanishing amid the storm.—
Nae man can tether time or tide;
The hour approaches *Tam* maun ride;   *must*
That hour, o' night's black arch the key-stane,   *turning point, of night's blackness*
That dreary hour he mounts his beast in;
And sic a night he taks the road in,   *such*
As ne'er poor sinner was abroad in.

The wind blew as 'twad blawn its last;   *would have blown*
The rattling showers rose on the blast;
The speedy gleams the darkness swallow'd;
Loud, deep, and lang, the thunder bellow'd:
That night, a child might understand,
The Deil had business on his hand.

Weel mounted on his gray mare, *Meg*,
A better never lifted leg,
Tam skelpit on thro' dub and mire,   *raced on*
Despising wind, and rain, and fire;
Whiles holding fast his gude blue bonnet;
Whiles crooning o'er some auld Scots sonnet;   *humming*
Whiles glowring round wi' prudent cares,   *gazing around with prudent carefulness*
Lest bogles catch him unawares: *goblins*
Kirk-Alloway was drawing nigh,
Whare ghaists and houlets nightly cry.—   *ghosts and owls*

By this time he was cross the ford,
Whare, in the snaw, the chapman smoor'd;   *pedlar smothered*
And past the birks and meikle stane,   *birches and the great stone*
Whare drunken *Charlie* brak 's neck-bane;   *broke*
And thro' the whins, and by the cairn,
Whare hunters fand the murder'd bairn;   *found*
And near the thorn, aboon the well,   *above*

Whare *Mungo*'s mither hang'd hersel.—
Before him Doon pours all his floods;
The doubling storm roars thro' the woods;
The lightnings flash from pole to pole;
Near and more near the thunders roll:
When, glimmering thro' the groaning trees,
Kirk-Alloway seem'd in a bleeze;   blaze
Thro' ilka bore the beams were glancing;   every gap
And loud resounded mirth and dancing.—

     Inspiring bold *John Barleycorn!*
What dangers thou canst make us scorn!
Wi' tippeny, we fear nae evil;   light ale
Wi' usquabae, we'll face the devil!—   whisky
The swats sae ream'd in *Tammie*'s noddle,   ale so frothed; head
Fair play, he car'd na deils a boddle.   he didn't give a farthing for devils
But *Maggie* stood right sair astonish'd,
Till, by the heel and hand admonish'd,
She ventured forward on the light;
And, vow! *Tam* saw an unco sight!   weird sight
Warlocks and witches in a dance;
Nae cotillion brent new frae *France*,   No; brought
But hornpipes, jigs, strathspeys, and reels,
Put life and mettle in their heels.
A winnock-bunker in the east,   window recess
There sat auld Nick, in shape o' beast;
A towzie tyke, black, grim, and large,   shaggy dog
To gie them music was his charge:
He screw'd the pipes and gart them skirl,   tuned; made them shriek
Till roof and rafters a' did dirl.—   shake
Coffins stood round, like open presses,   cupboards
That shaw'd the dead in their last dresses;   showed
And by some devilish cantraip slight   magic trick
Each in its cauld hand held a light.—
By which heroic *Tam* was able
To note upon the haly table,   holy
A murderer's banes in gibbet airns;   bones; irons
Twa span-lang, wee, unchristen'd bairns;   hand-span long
A thief, new-cutted frae a rape,
Wi' his last gasp his gab did gape;   mouth

Five tomahawks, wi' blude red-rusted;
Five scymitars, wi' murder crusted;
A garter, which a babe had strangled;
A knife, a father's throat had mangled,
Whom his ain son o' life bereft,   his own son killed
The grey hairs yet stack to the heft;   handle
Wi' mair o' horrible and awefu',
Which even to name wad be unlawfu'.

 As *Tammie* glow'rd, amaz'd, and curious,
The mirth and fun grew fast and furious:
The piper loud and louder blew;
The dancers quick and quicker flew;
They reel'd, they set, they cross'd, they cleekit, linked arms
Till ilka carlin swat and reekit,   every witch sweated and steamed
And coost her duddies to the wark,   shed her clothes to aid the work
And linket at it in her sark!   skipped; shift

 Now, *Tam*, O *Tam*! had thae been queans, young girls
A' plump and strapping in their teens, shirts; greasy linen
Their sarks, instead o' creeshie flannen,
Been snaw-white seventeen hunder linnen!
Thir breeks o' mine, my only pair,   trousers
That ance were plush, o' gude blue hair, once
I wad hae gi'en them off my hurdies, backside
For ae blink o' the bonie burdies!   one glance; beautiful girls

 But wither'd beldams, auld and droll, old women
Rigwoodie hags wad spean a foal,   withered old women who would wean a foal
Lowping and flinging on a crummock, leaping; crooked stick
I wonder didna turn thy stomach.

 But *Tam* kend what was what fu' brawlie, very well
There was ae winsome wench and wawlie, one; handsome
That night enlisted in the core,   crowd
(Lang after kend on *Carrick* shore; long after known
For mony a beast to dead she shot,   to death
And perish'd mony a bony boat,
And shook baith meikle corn and bear, destroyed great amount of corn and barley
And kept the country-side in fear:)

Her cutty sark, o' Paisley harn, *short shift of Paisley linen*
That while a lassie she had worn,
In longitude tho' sorely scanty,
It was her best, and she was vauntie.— *proud*
Ah! little kend thy reverend grannie, *knew*
That sark she coft for her wee Nannie, *bought*
Wi' twa pund Scots, ('twas a' her riches), *pounds*
Wad ever grac'd a dance of witches!

 But here my Muse her wing maun cour; *must lower her wing*
Sic flights are far beyond her pow'r;
To sing how Nannie lap and flang, *leapt and sprung*
(A souple jade she was, and strang), *supple bold girl; strong*
And how *Tam* stood, like ane bewitch'd,
And thought his very een enrich'd; *eyes*
Even Satan glowr'd, and fidg'd fu' fain, *twitched with excitement*
And hotch'd and blew wi' might and main:
Till first ae caper, syne anither, *one caper, then another*
Tam tint his reason a' thegither, *lost*
And roars out, 'Weel done, Cutty-sark!'
And in an instant all was dark:
And scarcely had he Maggie rallied,
When out the hellish legion sallied.

 As bees bizz out wi' angry fyke, *buzz out with angry fuss*
When plundering herds assail their byke; *herd-boys attack their hive*
As open pussie's mortal foes,
When, pop! she starts before their nose;
As eager runs the market-crowd,
When 'Catch the thief!' resounds aloud;
So Maggie runs, the witches follow,
Wi' mony an eldritch skreech and hollow. *uncanny screech and shout*

 Ah, *Tam*! Ah, *Tam*! thou'll get thy fairin! *reward*
In hell they'll roast thee like a herrin!
In vain thy *Kate* awaits thy comin!
Kate soon will be a woefu' woman!
Now, do thy speedy utmost, Meg,
And win the key-stane of the brig;
There at them thou thy tail may toss,

A running stream they dare na cross.
But ere the key-stane she could make,
The fient a tail she had to shake!   no tail at all
For Nannie, far before the rest,
Hard upon noble Maggie prest,
And flew at *Tam* wi' furious ettle;   purpose
But little wist she Maggie's mettle—   knew
Ae spring brought off her master hale,   brought her master off safely
But left behind her ain gray tail:
The carlin claught her by the rump,   witch; clutched
And left poor Maggie scarce a stump.

   Now, wha this tale o' truth shall read,   whoever reads this true tale
Ilk man and mother's son, take heed: each
Whene'er to drink you are inclin'd,
Or cutty-sarks run in your mind,
Think, ye may buy the joys o'er dear,   too dearly
Remember Tam o' Shanter's mare.

Tam o' Shanter completes our Burns selection; one of his greatest poems, and one of the world's most vivid supernatural tales, with astonishing pace and humour. We include it to round off since it shows Burns as the most attractive and humane of poets. It's familiar to all Burns lovers as a racy tale of the ordinary countryman who runs into trouble with witches and the devil – but do we perhaps miss just how subtle Burns is being? Isn't there another possible, more serious reading which could be summed up as 'the Presbyterian's nightmare'? Tam wants wine, women, song – all of which are off bounds to him since he must ride home. There are significantly two black arches in the poem which contain all the weird events of the night; the first, midnight, 'o' night's black arch the keystane', the traditional time for the supernatural to thrive – but perhaps for Tam the time when dozy with drink and fevered imagination, perhaps even unconscious on his faithful horse, he imagines or dreams what he wants – wine, women, song – in the old kirk of Alloway. But these are guilty pleasures, and so the Devil is at the back of it all, and Tam punishes himself for his guilty desires.

What do you think? Isn't there a sense in which Tam is a Scottish Everyman of the old Scotland, where pleasures are regarded as trivial and even morally wrong? And wouldn't that explain why Burns writes his lovely lines in English, reflective and so different from the rest of the poem, on how pleasure vanishes all too soon, 'like the snow upon the river'? Is he maybe saying that we Scots were a bit of a dour lot, incapable of letting go? Are we still like that? Notice that when Burns comes to warn us not to think on drink or 'cutty sarks' (shorthand for women), the penalty which is actually paid by Tam is the tail of his horse, escaping over the other arch in the poem, the bridge over the river Doon – and into reality again, as his sulky dame awaits...

This isn't to deny the story as a supernatural tale, only to suggest that there may be a parallel, but very different, interpretation *as well*. See what you think – and remember just how clever Burns could be!

Seamus Heaney

A Birl for Burns

From the start, Burns' birl and rhythm,
That tongue the Ulster Scots brought wi' them
And stick to still in Country Antrim
      Was in my ear.
From east of Bann it westered in
      On the Derry air.

My neighbours *toved* and *bummed* and *blowed*,
They *happed* themselves until it *thowed*,
By *slaps* and *stiles* they *thrawed* and *tholed*
      And *snedded thrissles*,
And when the rigs were *braked* and hoed
      They'd *wet their whistles*.

Old men and women getting crabbèd
Would hark like dogs who'd seen a rabbit,
Then straighten, stare and have a stab at
      Standard habbie:
Custom never staled their habit
      O' quotin' Rabbie.

Leg-lifting, heartsome, lightsome Burns!
He overflowed the well-wrought urns
Like buttermilk from slurping churns,
      Rich and unruly,
Or dancers flying, doing turns
      At some wild hooley.

For Rabbie's free and Rabbie's big,
His stanza may be tight and trig
But once he sets the sail and rig
      Away he goes
Like Tam-O-Shanter o'er the brig
      Where no one follows.

And though his first tongue's going, gone,
And word lists now get added on
And even words like *stroan* and *thrawn*
      Have to be glossed,
In Burns's rhymes they travel on
      And won't be lost.

Ask the world's most famous living English-language poet to write a poem in praise of the world's most famous Scots-language poet, living or dead… and away you go, Burns is reeled into the twenty-first century, as alive as he ever was in those marvellous poems.

Seamus Heaney's poem prefaces a collection of Burns's poems edited by Andrew O'Hagan, *A Night Out with Burns – the Greatest Poems.* Here you'll find Burns as lover, drinker, social critic, unmasking hypocrisy wherever he finds it, with a specially sharp eye on religion.

The Irish poet has already written with affection and understanding about the great modern bards of Scotland, Hugh MacDiarmid and Sorley MacLean. He composes his tribute to Burns using the 'Standard Habbie' that Burns popularised in poems such as 'To a Mouse', a verse form both lively and 'trig', as Heaney says. It lets the line out on a long lead then pulls it back in to make a point, heightened by rhyme or near-rhyme. It's a form that jogs the memory, as people gratefully find when they stand to recite Burns's poems in schools and community halls, in private clubs, in dining-rooms domestic and grand all over the world around 25th January.

The heart of Heaney's poem is not the personality of Burns, that 'antithetical mind' so memorably characterised by Lord Byron as 'Tenderness, roughness – delicacy, coarseness – sentiment, sensuality – soaring and grovelling – dirt and deity – all mixed up in that compound of inspired clay!' Here he celebrates the language of Burns, the tongue the Ulster Scots took with them to Ireland, still present in Heaney's childhood.

Yet is Heaney perhaps too quick to say it is 'going, gone', surviving as glossaries to Burns's poems where once it was in common usage? After all, 'thrawn' and 'tholed' are words often heard, pointing to aspects of the Scottish temperament whose opposite is a fondness for 'wild hooleys'. That 'first tongue' has survived and looks healthy. It may soon – thanks to energetic lobbying, not least by poets who continue to write in it – be admitted to equality with the other tongues of this diverse nation.

Heaney's poem suggests that the language of Burns, like the poet himself, is 'rich and unruly'. Burns has made work that cannot be contained in 'well-wrought urns', flying in the face of convention in his verse as in his life. The poet purifies the language of the tribe, T.S. Eliot said, but Burns rejoiced in its impurities, and because of his poems, they 'won't be lost'.

ROBYN MARSACK

Scots-English Glossary

aiblins perhaps
agley askew
amity friendship
at yince at once
awbody everybody
ay always

baet beat
bairntid childhood
baith both
barrie fine
beekin warming
bields shelter
bigg build
birl movement, dance
blate reluctant
blithe and blatter
happy and loud
blowed boasted
bocht bought
bogles hobgoblins
braid broad
breeks trousers
breid bread
breks breaks
bummed hummed

cadger pedlar, salesman
chitterin chattering
clam climb
clootie fit cloven foot
coorie huddle
cowp rubbish dump
crabbed bad-tempered
crambo doggerel
craitur creature

dargin dirr daily grind
dip steal from
ding doun lay low
dod o' oose speck
of fluff
dominies teachers
doo dove
dout believe
dowie dull
dreepin dripping
dreich dismal
dreh dry
drookit soaked through

eneuch enough
ettlin trying

fause false
fecht fight
fechtin fighting
feres, fieres companion,
friend
forgie forgive
fyle despoil, pollute

gallus extreme, bold
gart made to, forced
gawp gape
gear possessions
gey very, extremely
gied gave
gies gives
gin if
girnin complaining
glaikit dozy, daft
glede spark
gowks idiots, fools
graith equipment
greenie poles poles to
prop up washing lines
greetin crying,
moaning

hackit ugly
hame home
haly holy
happed wrapped
hauf droont half
drowned
hauns hands
hawked sold, borrowed
against
herrie plunder
hink think
hooley riot, wild party
hoose house
hunners hundreds
hurdies hips
inben within
ingles firesides

jinks dodges

kintra country

langsyne long ago
lave rest
lees lies
lour threaten
lowe glow
lowp leap

mair more
masel myself
maudlin miserable, sad
mercat market
megrim migraine
mense sense
mingin smelly
mirk gloom, dark
morra morning

oan ma tod by myself

paiks blows
ploo plough
pooches pockets
puckly few
puhl pull

ramfeezlet dazed by
exhaustion
rax stretch
rax yer haund reach out
your hand
redds cleans, clears
remeid remedy
reek smoke
rousty rusty
rowed rolled

saunds sands
scabbit barren,
worthless
scraich screech
selt sold
shair sure
sic such
sic a splore such an
uproar
skinkles glimmers
slaps passages, openings
sleekit sleek
smirr fine rain
snaw-bree melted
snow, slush

snedded cut off (the
tops)
soor mooth sour mouth,
gloomy person
speak language, way
of talking
stert start, beginning
stoating marvellous
stoury dusty
steekit stuck
straikt aff stroaked off,
creamed off
stroan drunk
swither confusion
syne then

tak tent take heed,
take care
tapmost highest
the morra tomorrow,
the future
thirled tied, chained
thole, tholed bear,
endure
thowed thawed
thrawed thrawn,
stubborn
threidbare threadbare
thrissles thistles
tight and trig
controlled and neat
toved gossiped
trauchled trod wearily

unsnecked unfastened

wad gar would force,
would make
waled chose
warld world
waukened awake
weans children
whaur where
weyoot without
wheen many, a lot

yett gate
yin one
yince once

Notes

This book is accompanied by a range of support materials. Individual notes firstly comment on Burns's poems, then the response poem. See also poets' commentaries and the glossary for further explanation.

Recommended books: Robert Crawford's new biography *The Bard: Robert Burns, A Biography* (2008); James Mackay's *Burns* (1992), and David Daiches's *Robert Burns* (1966). *Robert Burns* (2006) in the British Council's Writers and their work series, is a succinct and informative short study. An excellent short introduction for schools is Kenneth Simpson's *Robert Burns*, ASLS (1994).

See the BBC website for recordings of Burns's poems, and the LTS website for further Burns resources including lesson plans. See the Scottish Poetry Library website for information about contemporary poets.

www.bbc.co.uk/robertburns
www.ltscotland.org.uk/scotlandsculture
www.spl.org.uk/poets_a-z

To a Mouse / From a Mouse

Written around 1783, when Burns was working Lochlea Farm near Tarbolton, this could well have been thought of while Burns was actually ploughing. Its sadness may also owe something to the recent deaths of his father and ten-year-old brother John.

Liz Lochhead's poem argues from the point of view of the mouse (and a woman?); how far do you feel she is talking about Burns rather than the mouse? Is she fair to say that the mouse is 'artefact' – that is, something made for effect? Does she blame Burns for this – as well as his ways towards women?

Daphne Brown is the less glamorous sister of the *Sunday Post*'s cartoon 'The Broons'; Gray and Pope are Thomas Gray and Alexander Pope, famous 18th-century poets – find out more about them, and why Lochhead laughs at the idea of Burns as 'Heaven-taught'.

Lochhead talks in the third verse about Burns's uses of 'Standard Habbie', as arguably his favourite form of verse, as do several of the modern poets.

Lochhead uses it here herself; so what are its main features?

Lochhead closes with her mouse speaking ahead of its time, about global problems. What does she mean?

To a Louse / To a Louse

1784-5 Is Burns really talking to a louse? If not, who is he talking to, and what is he really saying?

The fifth verse refers to medicines – check the glossary for meaning. 'Miss's fine Lunardi' in the sixth verse is a name for her bonnet, named after a famous Italian balloonist. And note how in this poem, as so often in Burns, his poetry has given us a phrase or proverb which has passed into everyday use – can you spot it?

Is Tim Turnbull's poem more about Burns than the louse? Once again the modern poet asks, who is the real Burns – what do you find out from him? And what does Turnbull mean by calling him a 'proto-Thatcherite go-getter' in verse seven?

Rosenberg, Rimbaud, and Orwell are all writers – find out more, and why they are brought in here. St Andrews (verse six) is of course the Scottish university.

Poor Mailie's Elegy / Dead Otter

Burns wrote this at Lochlea, around 1783; it follows another comic lament, the mock elegy 'The Death and Dying Words of Poor Mailie', which will tell you more about Mailie and how she tangled herself in a rope and strangled herself. Such half-serious laments were popular in traditional Scottish poetry; but Mailie really was a favourite of Burns – so how far do you think Burns is serious, and how far joking, in the elegy itself?

The Gaelic poet Meg Bateman understands Burns's genuine sense of loss, but uses his poem as a link to the death of a very different and wild animal, the otter. How different is her poem from that of Burns in its attitude and tone?

Epistle to Davie / Epistle

1785 A manuscript note tells us that Davie (David Sillar) was 'a brother Poet, Lover, Ploughman and Fiddler'; he was a fellow-member of the Tarbolton Batchelor's Club which Burns helped to set up in 1780.

The poem is about two things; poverty and love. What is Burns saying about them, and how does Burns connect them?

Verse eleven refers to '*Phoebus* and the famous *Nine*', and to 'spavet *Pegasus*'; Phoebus is another name for Apollo, the Greek sun-God, leader of the nine muses, Goddesses of all the arts and sciences; Pegasus is the winged horse of Greek mythology, and seen as the inspiration of poetry. But why does Burns bring them in here, and why does he describe his horse of inspiration as 'spavet', or lame?

Notice the contrast in language between the completely standard English of verses nine and ten; and verse eleven, which drops back into Scots. How do you explain the difference? Like several of the response poems, Bill Herbert's 'Epistle' uses the Burns poem to comment on how Burns is treated now. His reference to Dr Grieve and MacDiarmid are to the same person, the great 20th century poet 'Hugh MacDiarmid', pen-name of Christopher Murray Grieve. Can you find out more about him and his poetry and why Herbert brings him in early in the poem?

Some of Herbert's vivid ideas are complex and surreal; you could discuss them in class and try to decide who are 'Haggismen' and 'maskless women', and what are their attitudes to Burns.

Herbert also refers to 'Lapraik'; you could look up the 'Epistle to John Lapraik: an Old Scottish Bard' as another fine example of Burns's natural and easy poetic letter-writing.

Epistle to a Young Friend / The Marble Quarry

1786 Robert Crawford's commentary gives a full account of the background to Burns's poem for young Andrew Aiken, and also discusses some of the inconsistencies between Burns's excellent advice and his (Burns's) own life practice! Look closely at the ending, however – doesn't Burns know all too well that he doesn't do what he says Andrew should?

Crawford's quiet and moving poem remembers a moment with his own son, in a very different time and place. What do you think are the main connections between the two poems?

Mary Morison / Sung

1781 It has been suggested that Mary Morison was actually Alison Begbie, daughter of a neighbouring farmer to Lochlea, who turned down Burns's offer of marriage. But does the reality matter, given the timelessness of this expression of troubled love?

Carol Ann Duffy's 'Sung' has much of Burns's quiet sadness, but uses the passage of time to suggest that all loves must pass… How would you manage to read out loud the last line of the first verse? Does this mean that the poem on the page is different from the spoken poem?

Duffy, as someone who left Scotland for England, gives another perspective on Burns, – so is Burns perhaps associated with another kind of loss in her poem?

A red red Rose / Rose

1793 Are this, 'Scots wha hae', and 'Auld Lang Syne' the most famous of all Burns poems and songs? Its folk-song simplicity and music sing for themselves. All the more striking, perhaps, is Matthew Fitt's response, 'Rose', where urban toughness and modern girlhood seem to mock such tender sentiments. But is this the case? Is something else going on behind the apparent hardness, something not ten thousand miles away from Burns?

John Anderson my Jo / Fiere

1790 Another example of Burns finding the absolute balance between simplicity and a universal and timeless declaration of ageless love, with the contrast of youth and age combining joy and sadness at the passage of time. Jackie Kay manages her own balance of youth and age in her contemporary celebration of fierce friendship. What is Jackie Kay saying about the difference between friendship and romantic love? How does she chart the passage of time?

Robert Bruce's March to Bannockburn (Scots wha hae…) / Aw Jock Tamson's

Burns wrote in 1793 to the song collector George Thomson that he was inspired by the thought that the old tune of 'Hey Tuttu Taitie' had been played as the Scots marched to war in 1314. Though this was not to be the present tune of 'Scots wha hae', it fired Burns to write 'on the theme of Liberty and Independence'.

Janet Paisley's response probably moves further away from Burns than the other modern poets here; but there are surely deep links between Burns's ideas of national independence and Paisley's ideas about modern loss of integrity and financial independence, as she shows her anger at our credit culture. How would you compare their attitudes?

Holy Willie's Prayer / Holy Gordon's Prayer

This savage satire on religious hypocrisy and bigotry, probably Burns's finest, had to be published anonymously in 1789, since its target, a self-righteous church elder, William Fisher, was very much alive. Burns's friend, lawyer Gavin Hamilton, was accused of neglecting his church duties; Robert Aiken successfully defended him in the Ayr Presbytery to Willie's rage. Like several of Burns's satires, it works by pretending to adopt the views of opponents, here in what is called a *dramatic monologue* – that is, the words are a speech like that of a play, and very far from the views of the Burns himself!

The poem deserves lengthy commentary; suffice it here to say that Burns manages in the first four verses to mock three of the crucial beliefs of hard-line Calvinism – belief in God's unknowable predestination of what happens to humanity; the doctrine of the Elect, that there are but a few chosen people that God has marked out to be saved from the very beginning, irrespective of their good or bad actions; and the notion of 'original sin', whereby Calvinists believed that we are all, even as new-born babies, in a state of sin, and worthy of Hell. We should fully recognise the sheer intelligence and wit of Burns and his audacity, in challenging such a powerful foe.

In 'Holy Gordon's Prayer' Rab Wilson provocatively links Holy Willie with Prime Minister Gordon Brown, in a detailed commentary on British politics in the days of Blair, and politicians across the world. This is the most challenging of our response poems; given limits of space here, it is left to you to find out the crises and problems for which poor Brown prays for God's help. There are a huge variety of issues here – and to make things more complex, Wilson gives biblical references throughout – which if you look them up will add even more satirical effect to the poem.

Address of Beelzebub / Beelzebub Resurfaces

See Robertson's commentary for background to this ferocious satire. It is another dramatic monologue from Hell's second-in-command, addressing London's Highland Society and in particular, the Earl of Breadalbane. In 1786 he met with landlords McKenzie of Applecross and McDonald of Glengarry to help them stop Applecross Highlanders from emigrating to Canada, as Burns says in his introduction, 'in search of that fantastic thing – LIBERTY'. (Burns's satire takes on added force, when we remember that only a few years later, many Highland landlords wanted nothing better than that their tenants emigrate…)

Again, space does not allow detailed explanation of all the named historical figures. John Hancock, Benjamin Franklin and George Washington (first president of the United States) were leaders of the American rebellion and the War of Independence against Britain in the 1770s; North and Sackville, Howe and Clinton, were British politicians and army generals opposing American independence, and thus seen by Burns as against all such freedom-seekers.

In the closing lines, Herod is probably Herod the Great, the first-century ruler of Palestine, famous for his cruelty, such as the Massacre of the Innocents at Bethlehem; Polycrates was the Greek Tyrant of Samos, around 522 BC; Diego de Almagro and Francisco Pizarro were sixteenth-century conquistadors, notorious for cruelty, leading the persecution of the Incas, and conquering Chile and Peru.

Note Beelzebub's dating of his address as 'HELL (the Year of the World) 5790'; Calvinists believed that Creation occurred less than six thousand years before 1786.

James Robertson connects Beelzebub in 1786 with Beelzebub 2009, imagining that since Hell is burnt out, our world is the best replacement, since we have made Paradise into 'a stinkin, scabbit cowp', with wars and global warming making it look as though Judgment Day has come. Burns may attack smaller problems, but can you find the connections between his and Robertson's poems?

A Birl for Burns

It seems appropriate to have a final poem from one of the greatest of modern poets, Irish Nobel Prize winner Seamus Heaney, one great poet paying tribute to another – and showing how Burns's language survives outside Scotland. Robyn Marsack, Director of the Scottish Poetry Library in Edinburgh, gives the commentary.